Dear World,

Don't Spin So Fast, I'm Having Trouble Hanging On

Joan
Wester
Anderson

ABBEY PRESS

St. Meinrad, Indiana 47577

Cover Design: Dwight Walles

Library of Congress Catalog Card Number
82-73131
ISBN: 0-87029-188-2

CONTENTS

WINTER

Dear Diary,

I found you under the Christmas tree this year, an unexpected gift from the child who always teases me about my scribbling. "Here, Mom," he presented it proudly. "You write so many notes and letters to other people, I thought you should write some to yourself, too."

He knows me well, this child. An inveterate letter writer, I seem to think more clearly when my words are set down on paper. But keeping a diary? I haven't done that since those dreamy high school days.

And as I ruffle through your pristine pages, I must admit to a sense of foreboding. Saying good-bye to an old year is not easy, for it represents time which has passed and will never come again. But at least I know what I am leaving behind; those experiences, joyful or disappointing, are over now, and just another part of the history our family continues to compile.

But starting a new year, and a new diary, seems infinitely more difficult, for your pages represent the unknown. What sorrows are looming on the horizon? What mistakes will be made? What events will you chronicle--will most be happy occasions? Or will I look back a year from now in regret for the time wasted, the dreams unrealized?

And yet as I flip through your pages, I remember that, like all diaries, you are broken into days, each a tiny but important fragment of the whole. And one day at a time is all that is asked of me, all that anyone can do.

It is not easy today, juggling the roles of wife, mother, daughter, employee, volunteer, friend--and

household inventory control specialist. Sometimes the
world spins much too fast--and I have trouble hanging
on. Where are my priorities? Whose need is greater?
What is expected of me? And why can't I ever find a
scissors in this house?

And yet I know that if I invite God into my life as a
Silent Partner, my burdens can be shared. And if I ask
him to hold my hand--just for today--that day will
multiply into a lifetime of happiness and hope.

And so, Diary, you will be my just-for-today record.
Just for today, with God's help, I'll be patient and
serene (tomorrow I'll kick the clothes drier). Just for
today I'll cope in the best way I know how, trusting
that the path will be made clearer as time goes on. Just
for today I'll write my thoughts to you (tomorrow I
may not be able to locate a pencil) and toss you into the
drawer where so much of my correspondence is kept.

Just for today, Diary, be my confidant, reflect my
feelings, accept me as I am. It is the only day we have.

Love,
Me

Dear TV Weatherman,

Enough, already! Is it really necessary to preface each ten o'clock news program with films of pedestrians slowly disappearing into snowbanks, or bumper-to-bumper blobs chugging their perilous slippery way down ice-encrusted tollways? I realize that this is reality, but aren't you really overdoing it just a bit?

First of all, as a person who is frozen solid from the end of every October right through the beginning of May (no matter how many afghans I'm wearing), I find nothing exciting in the constantly reported fact that our windchill factor is now a minus 73.

I also do not appreciate the five-second news blurbs interspersed throughout each hour, such as: "Biggest snow on record now forecast. Hoarding, looting, and power failures predicted. Details at ten." What is one to do with this information during the next ninety minutes? Should I sift through my remaining food supply? Walk the dog one last time? Make out my will? Or retreat behind the furnace to suck my thumb? If we have to be reminded of a raging blizzard accompanied by ten-foot-high tidal waves and tornado spin-offs, can't you wait at least until it starts before discussing same?

These titillating tags also have an adverse effect on my children, Mr. Weatherman. As you can imagine, I have brought them up to understand that their main responsibility in life is to get a good education (and not ask Mother any questions). But how can a child settle down to a serious homework session when she knows full well that if the drifts get any deeper, the school will probably declare a snow holiday--and announce it first, of course, on Station PHEW. It's becoming a real battle to force the children into bed before the midnight news wrap-up. And twice this week I've discovered the eight year old on his knees at four AM, praying in front of the test pattern. I wish you could explain to me why children are able to rouse themselves before dawn on a snow holiday, but must be dragged from under the covers at least a dozen times when classes are going to be in session.

I would appreciate it, too, if your film crew would refrain from taking pictures of tanned bodies cavorting in the Florida surf, and then cutting to a local shot of neighborhood kids having "fun" on ski slopes and sleds. Instead, for real in-depth reporting, how about a shot of the kids' mother as she unwraps the three year old for the third time in ten minutes because he "hasta go bafroom" again, or tries to figure out where to dry seven pairs of rubber boots, or attempts to unload a week's worth of groceries from a station wagon that just skidded onto the neighbor's patio? Winter may have its charms but, frankly, I find nothing enchanting about a backyard snowman who's been standing there like a rock since the Thanksgiving holidays. Unless you're prepared to put the entire northern and midwest housewife population on charter planes to Jamaica, please spare us the scenes of what our southern sun-baked neighbors must endure.

Actually, I'm on to your system, Mr. Weatherman. What better way to justify the importance of your job at PHEW than with room-sized charts and graphs, automated hurricanes, on-the-scene interviews with rainmakers, and induced hysteria over each change in the cloud formations? Someone has to be reminded that you deserve attention and respect--and many pay it willingly. But as for me, I'm getting somewhat crotchety in my mid-life cycle and have decided to forego the nightly course in meteorology. From now on, I'll either open a window or let my rheumatism be my guide.

Happy predicting (without me),
Mrs A.

January 6

Acme Building and Remodeling Company

Gentlemen:

Thank you for your recent estimate on remodeling our upstairs bathroom. As I mentioned to your salesman when he came to measure the room, we have saved this project for last since we realize that it is going to be quite a challenge.
However, I do think he overreacted a bit--I'm not used to grown men bursting into tears just because our bathtub is a little uneven and the shower rod has to be kept on with Scotch tape.
Frankly, my husband thinks your bid of $9000 for a 6' x 8' room is slightly steep, so we will look elsewhere.

January 8

Better Builders, Inc.

Gentlemen:

Your recent bathroom remodeling estimate of $8000 is appreciated, but not quite what we had in mind. I do hope your salesman has recovered from the concussion caused by the medicine cabinet falling on his head. (Our insurance company will be in touch.)
Please tell him we have considered his original suggestion, that of burning the bathroom down, but feel there must be a better way.

January 11

Continental Building Corporation

Gentlemen:

Your salesman may think he has a devastating sense of humor, but suggesting that we remodel the rest of the house before tackling the bathroom did not sit well with my husband--who has spent the last six years on a ladder doing same.
I have never heard of a company refusing a project on the grounds of "cruel and unusual punishment" but if that's the way you feel about it, we don't want your business either!

January 14

Delphinium Contracting Company

Gentlemen:

Your recent bathroom remodeling bid of $7900 is within our budget, but only if we all stop eating for the next two years. I am well aware that a toilet which moves across the floor presents some special plumbing challenges (and the large hole in the wall should obviously have a window in it) but, after all, you people are supposed to be the experts. . . .

January 17

Memo to Husband

By pooling bank loans, savings accounts, and the kids' piggy banks, I have been able to accumulate $107.00

toward supplies for the upstairs bathroom. Your
ladder, paint brushes, and blasting powder are in the
garage.
We'll be living at mother's for the duration, Dear. Call
us when the bathroom's finished.

Dear Mom,

So glad to hear that you and Dad have settled in happily under that Arizona sunshine. It's going to be a long six weeks for the rest of us (and I'm still amazed at how quickly you made the decision to leave) but you both deserve an extended vacation away from this horrid weather.

That nice Mrs. Peterson from your building phoned here yesterday to get your address. Although she's going to miss you, she says, she's really rather glad to get a break from your organ playing. Her husband apparently put so much cotton in his ears that he had to have it surgically removed in the hospital emergency room last week. Actually, I can't imagine your playing ''Chopsticks'' for twelve consecutive hours, so I can only conclude that that son of mine has been at it again. Honestly, Mom, you don't have to let him spend all day Sundays over at your place. Or at least you could close the windows.

Well, anyway, things are lively here. When you left, I was knee-deep in committee work for our upcoming school reunion, and by the time I track down all our missing classmates I'll probably have to have surgery to remove the telephone receiver from my ear. Remember Mickey O'Mara? The boy who drove a Good Humor truck down the church's middle aisle? The kid who used to tape **Playboy** centerfolds onto the front of the teacher's desk? I had a terrible time locating him. Obviously, I checked all the reform school alumni lists right away and even asked the warden of our state penitentiary to go through his files. No luck. It was as if Mickey had vanished from the face of the earth.

His invitation must have finally caught up with him, though, because yesterday he sent me a very nice note from Washington, D.C. He won't be able to make the reunion because he's conducting a high-level strategy session that weekend at the Pentagon. Isn't it funny how things turn out?

By the way, Mom, the service station phoned to say that your car probably won't be fixed for another month. Why didn't you tell me that my daughter stuffed an ice-cream cone down the air conditioning vent? Honestly, you don't have to take her for a ride every Saturday just because she howls her head off and threatens to turn blue. And here I thought you decided to take a plane because it was more convenient.

We're going to be godparents for Barbara Becker's new baby, and I couldn't be more pleased. It's a real honor to be part of a baptism for a twelfth child (or maybe they were just running out of people to ask). Anyway, Barb knows how I hate crowds, so she's keeping it simple--just an after-christening get-together for her family and ours. Just the immediate 21 of us. Barb still looks wonderful, and I don't know how she does it. I'd give anything to weigh 85 pounds again.

Oh, and speaking of weight, your high school grandsons really miss all your homemade goodies. But honestly, Mom, you don't have to bake each of them his own cake every time they come. They can darn well split one, the way they do around here. And about the matter of your broken TV screen--I'm sorry I didn't hear about it until after you left, but we will definitely have it repaired for you.

That's about it for now, Mom. You and Dad soak up every sun-filled moment out there. And we'll be counting the days until your return.

Love and kisses,
Your daughter

Dear Mrs. Parker,

It was delightful to receive your note (I haven't had a fan letter in two years, except from my mother), and I'm happy that you enjoyed reading my article, "Icky-looking Rashes" in **Baby Health** Magazine. You ask how I launched my free-lance writing career, and whether I have any tips for beginners.

Actually, Mrs. Parker, I wish I could say that I started writing out of a desire to help mankind or, at the very least, to fulfill my inner creative urgings. Unfortunately, neither motivation was mine. I had just read about a woman who began to write because she hated housework. The more sales she made, the more often she could afford to hire a cleaning lady to do her housework so she could write more and sell more, so the lady could clean more, so she could write more . . . well, you get the idea. In addition, we were in the middle of a do-it-yourself redecorating project, and since my husband and I weren't speaking to each other anyway, I figured I might as well do something constructive with all that silence. One thing led to another and now, some nine years later, I've published hundreds of articles, several books, and also lecture to women's clubs (the farther from home, the better). I never did hire the cleaning lady--my income goes for more luxurious items such as orthodontia, tuition, and meat--but I still think of her, wistfully, from time to time.

Free-lance writing, while surrounded by a family which is more interested in your production of meals and clean clothes than your production of articles, can be a bit difficult. But from my experience, I've garnered a few hints which you might appreciate:

Material Guidebooks tell you that indispensable tools for the would-be writer include several freshly sharpened pencils, a small notebook for jotting down ideas and clever phrases, and a typewriter, well-oiled and preferably bolted to the desk. Along with these necessities I would add a telephone disconnector, handy for turning off the incessant jangling when you wish to get some work done, and a sturdy door lock, which will keep you protected against the onslaught of children demanding that you settle their arguments that immediately break out whenever you reach for a pencil.

Practice Teachers of creative writing classes usually advise that you write something every day in order to keep your skills finely honed. I have noticed, however, that teachers of creative writing classes rarely write anything themselves or, if they do, are able to practice their craft in the creative confines of a quiet library or underneath a solitary old oak tree, dripping with creativity. For those of us in less ideal circumstances, the write-every-day theory is still valid but must be somewhat tempered; notes to your milkman and those extremely creative missives to the school principal do count.

Ideas According to writer-mentors of today, a budding free-lancer must learn to open her senses to the world around her, become aware of the dance of sights and the music of sounds which will stimulate the creation of poetic phrases and inspiring rhetoric. But to me, there's not much "music" in a toddler's 2 AM crying jag. And opening my senses to the sight and smell of stale socks under the bed may provoke an attack of nausea, but not much else.

Instead, family conversations provide journalistic grist for me. Overhearing my husband remark, "I've got nothing against women drivers, provided they stay off the road," may lead to a rather compelling article on Male Chauvinist Pigs. (It may also lead to a rather spirited discussion.) And when the children moan, "Oh, no, not tuna again!" I can always turn another dinnertime disaster into a treatise on the difference between democracy and dictatorship. As you can see, the possibilities are endless.

Writing, Mrs. Parker, is a profession that requires determination and stick-to-itiveness, but unlike my sisters employed in the Outside World, I have little or no job overhead (carbon paper is cheap) and am not required to wear shoes. I can take my work with me wherever I go (I've scribbled in department store restrooms while the kids tried on jeans, composed on a park bench while someone finished Toddler Swim Class, on airplanes on my way to give a speech, in the bathroom with the shower running). Writing is also versatile--I've taught adult ed. courses, done editing and proofreading for local businesses, and even gotten out of coaching Girls' Soccer by volunteering to write their publicity instead.

Thus, if you'd like to launch a journalistic career, Mrs. Parker, the best way to do it is just to jump in and swim with the rest of us. And in case you run into writer's block, just do what I do: Write letters instead.

Sincerely,
JA

February 2

Dear Mrs. Fraser,

It's been a whole semester, and my son is apparently adjusting well to third grade. (That is, you haven't sent home any threatening notes, and I always operate on the theory that no news is definitely good news.) However, there is one problem that I would like to discuss with you.

Mrs. Fraser, I do not sew. I was the only student in sophomore home ec. to flunk Needle Threading. My husband's favorite blue shirt has been without cuff buttons since 1974. If something rips around our house, my children wouldn't dream of pointing it out to me--they still remember the year I tried to make a throw pillow, and ended up with a three-legged diaper.

Moreover, I am not creative with sequins or spray paint. I do not get my jollies by gluing gumdrops onto cardboard cutouts and have discovered a latent allergy to papier-mâché.

Having thus been informed, Mrs. Fraser, I am hoping that you will exercise restraint when casting my son in any school play requiring a homemade costume.

Of course, you remember the recent Nativity play (although I'm sure the entire faculty is trying to forget). Assigning my son the role of sheep dog was a stroke of genius as far as the script was concerned. (What third grader wouldn't relish shrieking, "Arf, arf!" at three-minute intervals throughout the performance?) But the required "wooly costume" left me feeling befuddled and inferior, as usual. Other mothers would have concocted a realistic number, I'm sure, given a few moments with a scissors and an old black shag rug. But I own neither item and, in a moment of desperation, I whipped Little Sister's brown-and-white bedspread out of the hamper and informed Son he was going as a beagle. (Personally, I thought sending along the stew bone was a clever gesture--how was I to know the kids would use it as a baseball? Our insurance company should have contacted you by now on the broken windowpane.)

Anyway, you know the rest. As Little Sister and I sat in the audience, she spotted Son wearing her bedspread, leaped off my lap onto the stage, and dragged it off his back just as the angels were being lowered by pulley for the Grand Finale. Actually, I thought it added a nice touch--after all, Jesus said, "Let the little children come unto me"--but I quite understand why you felt compelled to lock yourself into the supply room and spend the rest of the day weeping into a pile of paper clips.

Then there was the school's celebration honoring "Know Your Nutrients" month. Word has it that some fortunate children were assigned roles as cabbages or bananas, allowing their mothers to simply hunt up an old green or yellow jump suit and be done with it. But how, pray tell, does one dress as a carbohydrate?

Like any conscientious parent, I keep a large box of ragged wearing apparel suitable for school plays, Halloween, and days when I run out of laundry soap. But somehow, neither the sombrero, Raggedy Ann wig, nor swim fins seemed to capture the essence of a nutrient.

So I regret that you feel my final decision was, in your words, "a royal cop-out," but I see nothing wrong with Son wearing a large sign stating, "I am a carbohydrate." At least the audience got the message.

Now, according to your latest note, the class is observing Healthy Feet Week. Again, I feel your costume request is a bit much. My neighbor's daughter is going as a toe, and perhaps with a giant-sized bottle of nail polish, I might have been able to handle that assignment. Even the kid down the block, who portrays a saddle shoe, gets off easily--white shirt and pants with a brown cummerbund (and shoelaces braided through his hair) ought to do the trick. But frankly, I'm tired of the other mothers' pitying stares when I reveal Son's part. No one has the slightest idea what a bunion should properly wear.

Next play, could you consider allowing my son to be the curtain-puller? Or better yet, absent?

Clumsily yours,
Brian's Mommy

Dear God,

As You know, I've just returned home from the doctor's office with yet another small flu victim. Tonight stretches ominously before me, endless hours of temperature taking, bed changing, and weary little voices quavering, "Mommy?" in the darkness.

I never appreciate healthy robust children until they are suddenly transformed into wistful, wan shadows, lying on couches with tissue boxes and tired eyes. Worse, I don't even welcome the fact that this is temporary--and that some parents must struggle with the heartache of an illness that never ends. No, instead, I grumble, complain, and stagger through alcohol rubs, sleepless nights, and rising pharmacy bills. Help me, Father.

Help me to accept with grace and understanding this detour in my routine. Let me serve my children with kindness and be what they most need me to be--a pleasant, reassuring mommy.

Remind me that your Son ministered to the leper, fed the hungry, comforted the sorrowing, and has asked us to do the same. Give me the strength to follow in his footsteps.

I know winter must be good for something, Father, because you made it. Now help me to accept the flu season as one more mysterious blessing in your loving plan for me.

Your impatient but loving child

February 12

Dear George, Abe, and Val,

My kids are hero-worshipers. They're impressed with the tales of the saints, particularly those early Christians who earned their fame by defying lions. My gang is also reduced to awe-struck silence at the sight of any professional athlete. They are not discriminatory--a trampoline bouncer competing for the county finals receives the same open-mouthed admiration as Chris Evert Lloyd or Walter Payton.

Then, of course, there are local heroes. My fifth-grade boy scout idolizes his scoutmaster who can start a fire with one match. My freshman reveres a classmate, appropriately named Piggy MacPherson, who can eat four bag lunches in third hour Mechanical Drawing and still have room left for the school cafeteria's Dessert of the Day. My daughter is impressed with her grandmother, who can out-hopscotch most of the kids on our block.

With all this reverence floating around, one would assume that heroic qualities would naturally rub off on my brood, that they would be wiser, better behaved, more organized, or at least cleaner, because of their attraction to these stellar figures. Alas, such is not the case, and at no time is this dismal situation more obvious than during February, when a star-studded calendar provides a host of luminaries for my kids to imitate. If only they would. . . .

Memo to you, George Washington: Yesterday, my daughter came home from school to announce a forthcoming day off.

"How come?" I asked.

"I dunno," she shrugged, tossing her books in a

plate of spaghetti I had just dished up for her high-school brother (the one whose work schedule demands early dinners on Tuesdays and Thursdays). "It's somebody's birthday who ate a lot of cherries once."

"Oh, the guy with the ax?" asked Fifth Grader. "I think that's Saint Potomac or somebody. . . ."

George, where have I gone wrong? Why haven't your sterling qualities rubbed off on my gang? Haven't I spent the last several Februarys cutting leotards into reasonable imitations of eighteenth-century garb for costumes in school plays? Wasn't it, in fact, one of my sons who once excitedly lisped on stage: "I cannot tell a lie--I did it!" And wasn't it this same kid who later, when presented with the remains of a chocolate cake, screamed, "Gosh, Ma--I didn't eat it! How come you're always picking on me?" (He just wears those cake crumbs on his cheeks for decoration, I guess.)

And another problem, George--when my kids do imitate one of your actions, they usually put the wrong interpretation on it. Frankly, I'm not sure why you found it necessary to toss those coins across the river, but do you think you can reassure my gang that maintaining a savings account is not against the law? They can't hold onto cash long enough to lose it, not with all the bubble gum, pizza, designer jeans, doll clothes, and comic books tempting them. "You kids are throwing your money to the four winds," I once grumbled.

"If it was good enough for George" the ten year old began sweetly.

"Never mind."

Then there's the matter of Patrick Henry, a pal of yours who went around spouting quotable remarks at the drop of a three-cornered hat. I admit his words still have a certain ring to them, but not when they are used by a sixteen year old who just got his driver's license.

"You were an hour late again tonight!" I stormed at my erring hot-rodder (who should be home from his Monday and Wednesday job by 9 PM). "What am I going to do with all this dried-up spaghetti? One more slipup, Pal, and you'll be grounded!"

Son drew himself into an impressive pose. "Give me liberty or give me death!" he intoned grandly, and then peered at me. "Well?"

"Don't rush me," I told him. "I'm thinking it over."

Memo to you, Abraham Lincoln: I've always been impressed with the fact that you once walked several miles to return a borrowed book. I'm wondering, therefore, if you could convince my children that there's merit in following your example. Yesterday, while excavating their bedrooms, I came across four copies of **The Wonderful World of Kidneys** and two **Know Your White Rat**, all due last September. At five cents per day per copy, including compound interest, well, I'll let you figure it out.

Memo to St. Valentine: Love is great, but does it have to include chocolate hearts ground into the rug? Quarrels over who will use my scissors to cut the lace from my best pillowcase for an extraspecial card? Bow and arrow lessons for a kid who's playing Cupid--literally--for his sister and her steady? Paste and red paper scraps on the leaves of my begonia?

Frankly, fellows, all this hero worship is driving me crazy. Can't you talk it over among yourselves and come up with a reasonable solution to my problem? Oh, and when you do, you'll find me in the kitchen. Husband has an eight o'clock meeting, Little Sister gets home from tap-dancing class at six, the two high schoolers are leaving at 6:30 for choir practice--and they all like their spaghetti hot.

In joyful celebration,
Mrs. A

Dear Donna,

Congratulations on becoming a mother! I thought your personally designed birth announcement--a pair of crossed safety pins superimposed on a background of strained rhubarb--was exceptionally clever. You always were my most talented cousin.

You asked for advice on adjusting to this new life, and commented "Thank goodness, the worst part is over!" Donna, I hardly know how to break this to you, but your duty time logged in the labor and delivery rooms was a Ferris wheel ride compared to what awaits you now. Despite the impression you may have gathered from watching "Brady Bunch" reruns, most children are not perpetually well-mannered, well-groomed--or even well, for that matter. (And most homes do not contain a maid who regards 24-hour-a-day service as her solemn obligation and privilege.)

No, like the rest of us, you will travel this long and interesting maternal road alone, stopping only for bits of advice or solace from those you meet along the way. Finding myself several miles ahead of you on the journey, I can only offer a few principles which may guide you through this first year with Baby:

1. It is an unwritten law that if an infant has kept you up all night with colic, and finally falls into a deep sleep right after breakfast (thus enabling you to grab a little shut-eye), your telephone will ring four times before 9:30 AM. In addition, the local encyclopedia salesman will choose that morning to display his wares and your next-door neighbor will have a grease fire in her kitchen, thus supplying plenty of noisy excitement on your front lawn.

2. Washing machines break down only after a mother has grabbed the last clean undershirt and stretch suit from Baby's drawer.

3. Guard against becoming too smug about your cherub's early accomplishments, for time is the Great Equalizer. The baby who sits up at three months and walks soon after, will still be demanding a pacifier during kindergarten registration; the angel who learns her ABCs before her first birthday will also develop the meanest karate chop in the neighborhood.

4. You will receive loads of adorable gifts for the baby; however, no one will give you what you need most--a dozen sponges, four pairs of earplugs, and a giant-sized bottle of aspirin.

5. Husbands who throughout the pregnancy have mouthed high-sounding phrases about parenting being a "dual responsibility" will suddenly remember a prior engagement when faced with a suspiciously-full diaper.

6. Contrary to popular theory, a four month old has no preconceived opinion on the correct order of a meal; therefore, mixing a little chocolate pudding into the strained spinach-and-liver is only common sense.

7. Refrain from blithely throwing a rubber ducky or a plastic fish into the sterilizer. Likewise, beware of becoming overly-conscientious about dirt--a crawling baby who occasionally drinks out of the dog's water dish will not contract Bubonic Plague.

8. A baby carriage parked under a shady backyard tree will attract plenty of mosquitoes, small kids, and stray dogs. It will not, however, attract a volunteer to push it so that you may shampoo and blow-dry your hair in only one operation.

9. A precious bundle who has spent the past four days chuckling in her jump chair, gurgling rapturously at any passing shadow, will launch a two-hour screaming fit as soon as her grandma, godmother, or assorted great-aunts come to visit.

10. Left to his own devices, a growing infant eventually works his way into two daily naps. The only problem is that one nap will occur during lunchtime, and the second, right around supper. During his wakeful hours he will, of course, be ravenous.

11. Learn to child-proof your home once Little Miss Adorable starts to get around. Utilize gates, outlet covers, and especially the playpen (it's a great place to get your mending done).

12. When taking a baby on a cross-country auto trip, leave the stuffed bunnies at home and opt for practical items only. Pack sunglasses, some interesting novels, aspirin, and for Baby, a large supply of paper towels, thus avoiding pit stops for diaper changes.

13. A curious creeper who has accidentally swallowed a goldfish will not develop fins.

14. Forget about educational toys (and also the baseball mitt your husband brought home as a christening gift). Junior will learn everything he needs to know by banging your pots and pans together, eating stale bread crumbs off the carpet, and flipping that small latch on the inside of the bathroom door.

15. It is an unwritten law that an almost one year old's affection for his evening bottle increases in direct proportion to his mother's repugnance for said bottle; that the harder a proud parent searches for that first tooth, the later it will erupt; that a baby would much rather chew his first pair of hard-soled shoes than wear them.

16. It is also an accepted theory that nothing in this world is more beautiful, more fulfilling, and more worthwhile than a baby--especially when he is yours.

Enjoy every minute of this coming year, Donna. You'll never have another one quite like it!

Love,
The Voice of Experience

February 1-March 8

Monday, February 1

Dear Coach Riley,

   Please excuse my son Tim from swimming class this week. He has an ear infection.

Sincerely,
Mrs. A.

Monday, February 8

Dear Coach Riley,

   Please excuse my son Tim from swimming class this week. He has an ingrown toenail.

Sincerely,
Mrs. A.

Monday, February 15

Dear Coach Riley,

   Please excuse my son Tim from swimming class this week. He has pains in his chest.

Sincerely,
Mrs. A.

Monday, February 22

Dear Coach Riley,

Please excuse my son Tim from swimming class this week. He is trying a new brand of acne medication.

Sincerely,
Mrs. A.

Monday, March 1

Dear Coach Riley,

Please excuse my son Tim from swimming class this week. He is suffering from tennis elbow.

Sincerely,
Mrs. A.

Monday, March 8

Dear Coach Riley,

I have just received Tim's report card and feel that his "F" in swimming class is totally unwarranted. I realize that he has not entered the pool this quarter, but if he is ever well enough to do so, you will discover that he can perform an admirable Australian crawl, not to mention floating on his back for over two minutes.

Perhaps you and I should have a conference.

Not so sincerely,
Mrs. A.

March 9

Dear Amy,

It has been a long winter for us housebound hausfraus, hasn't it? Only the class reunion helped to stem our cabin fever. You looked so classy in those penny loafers--wish I had thought to save mine.

I'm glad, despite the revelry, that we got a chance to have a long talk, but you did ask a question (toward the end of the evening) which I didn't have a chance to discuss. You asked (accompanied by another round of Chablis) what is the purpose of motherhood.

Well, Amy, we mothers wear a variety of hats, which we put off and on faster than the speed of sound.

To the TV pitchmen we are household drudges who become ecstatic over shiny floors or spend our afternoons dancing with the Pillsbury doughboy.

To the lady in charge of the Clean Sewers Committee we are warm bodies--women who don't "work," and who will therefore jump at the chance to canvass our neighborhood for signatures or funds.

To the grocery store manager we are a sea of blue jeans, converging weekly in checkout lines to gossip, gripe about prices, and chase toddlers through a nine-foot-high display of cotton balls.

To our children's teachers we are a quivering mass of neuroses, hunched knees-to-chin in miniature desks while trying to explain why James has not turned in any math homework since October.

To our husbands we are life-partners, doggedly holding up our end of the "Better or Worse" bargain; to our parents, the Younger Generation; to our physicians, a collection of aging tissues and varicose veins.

But only our kids are able to cut through the confusion of multiple hats and see us moms for what we truly are. They alone realize our true reason for being: Mothers were created to answer questions.

Over the years it has been made quite clear to me by my offspring that answering questions is my main function in life. But like many women, I did not realize my calling immediately; I had to be led into it on a gradual basis starting, as I recall, when my eldest was about three.

"How high is the sky?" he asked one day, pointing a chubby finger heavenward.

"Very high." I smiled fondly at his obviously superior intellect.

"Why?"

"Why what?"

"Why is the sky very high?"

"Well, . . ." I frantically searched my memory for Dr. Spock's guidelines-for-impossible-situations and came up blank. "I suppose because God made it that way."

"Does God live on the other side of the sky, Mommy?"

"He sure does."

"Then why did you say he lives in church?"

"Have a doughnut, Sweetheart."

As my second son also developed the marvelous power of speech, I found myself constantly badgered.

"What do you think Audrey is having for breakfast this morning, Mom?" (Audrey being a distant relative who lives across the world.)

"I don't have the faintest idea, Honey."

"Do you think she is having cereal?"

"She probably is."

"Then how come you said you didn't know?"

Like it or not, I had discovered my calling. Henceforth, I was to be the household Dispenser of All

Knowledge, ready and able to expound at the drop of a doughnut on Major League batting averages, the motives of classroom teachers, or weather conditions in any given part of the universe. "Is it snowing right now in Toronto?" "What would happen if I jumped off the chimney?" "Why is your hair getting gray?" were only a few of the daily skirmishes I learned to endure during my on-the-job training years.

As my offspring grew, however, I discovered their Master Plan: I was to be substituted for a twenty-volume set of Encyclopedia Britannica. As Brain Trust in Residence, I was expected to be well-versed in the mating habits of African ants, 17 times 12 squared (doubled, redoubled, and vulnerable), and whether Zanzibar's prime export is lettuce or peppermint. "Why don't you kids look that stuff up at the library?" I bellowed one day. "What am I--some sort of walking Einstein? How am I supposed to know when dinosaurs became extinct?"

"Gosh," one child murmured to another, "doesn't she ask a lot of questions?"

Another unfortunate aspect of being an oracle is that we moms must know the constant whereabouts of approximately nine thousand items of clothing, toys, sports equipment, school notes, and household miscellany. No matter where my children drop their belongings, they are confident that Know-It-All Mom will keep a mental log of each hiding place.

"Do you know where my bike lock is, Mom?"

"Have you looked in all the obvious places--under the couch, on top of the cookie jar, inside the piano bench?"

"Yep, here it is--buried in the hanging planter. Thanks, Mom, you're a genius." So what else is new?

I've managed to survive the early and middle years of kid raising by hanging on to one thought: when they become teenagers they will have all the answers, and no one will ever ask me anything again. My oldest sons are in high school now, but unfortunately only part of my premise is true. My adolescents do know everything there is to know about current clothing fads, rock artists, proper hair length, reasonable curfews, how often they should have custody of the car, and why Dad is putting on a few pounds. What they do not know (and thus query me about at least 40 times a day) is the state of our refrigerator.

"Can I eat this cake, Mom?"

"Put that back--it's for dinner."

"When's dinner?"

"Half an hour."

"What are we having?"

"Cake."

"Well then, can I drink this gallon of milk?"

There are advantages to being a perpetual Fountain of Wisdom; the chore keeps a mother mentally alert and physically fit. (I can leap a flight of stairs in five seconds flat anytime I overhear a child muse, "Wonder what would happen if I flush this down the toilet.")

But unfortunately, not every question has an answer. And that's why I've spent the past two weeks sifting through textbooks and dialing information services around the country. Someone must be able to tell me how long it takes a giraffe to swallow. After all, I owe it to the kids.

Hope this solves your dilemma, Amy. If it doesn't, there are two alternatives open to you. Turn all questions over to your husband, or join a macrame class (preferably one which meets five evenings a week) and just forget the whole thing.

See you at our next reunion. Can't wait to see if you really do locate those old argyle socks.

Love,
Me

March 13

Dear Internal Revenue Service,

I'm not the first taxpayer who has ever complained about the ridiculous pittance allowed for dependent deductions, nor will I be the last. You're well used to folks pointing out that $750 per annum will barely cover a teenage daughter's cosmetics bill, much less keep a normal average son in meat and milk (to say nothing of double-knee jeans). So I won't say it again. Instead I'll ask you to consider the hidden expenses involved in raising a child--and explain to me just where these deductions should be itemized on our annual return.

--Seventeen 30-amp fuses, used during a seventeen-day period in July, when the fifth-grader continuously turned the air conditioner from ''Low'' to ''High'' without passing through ''Medium.''

--Karate lessons for a son who needed to come out of his shell (and who, having eventually done so, now needs lessons in tact, judgment, and the civil rights of others).

--Six broken bowls, a burned-out mixer, and a chipped kitchen floor tile, the result of one middle-sized daughter and her friend attempting to bake a surprise angel food cake for Mom. (Do we get to deduct the cake, too? It weighed eleven pounds, but the bowling alley disqualified it for use in competition due to the too-large center hole.)

--Twelve algae eaters, a particularly loathsome type of fish whose duty is to keep the sides of a child's aquarium free of that yucky green stuff. (I might suggest that Congress launch an investigation into the appalling death rate of said fish--perhaps it's something in the environment, but ours never seem to make it from one payday to the next).

--Fifteen dollars' worth of postage stamps, purchased for our Christmas cards which the toddler, in a burst of holiday helpfulness, pasted onto the back of the clothes drier.

--My husband's collection of Revolutionary War coins, which our four year old inadvertently dropped into vending machines all over town.

--My husband's collection of screwdrivers, nails, and hammers, which our ten year old inadvertently left scattered throughout the yard (rusted) and the driveway (run over).

--My husband's collection of clothes, which our sixteen year old inadvertently left spattered with ketchup stains or languishing in the high school's Lost and Found department.

--One small dog, acquired to teach the kids responsibility (and also acquired because no one could resist her rather mournful eyes) who, over the course of this year, required three sets of puppy shots, two sets of collars and leashes, a blue water dish molded in the shape of a beef bone, several decent slippers on which to teethe, a perfectly good coffee table leg on which to teethe, three beds (all of which she rejected in favor of the ten year old's sleeping bag), a gallon of disinfectant to cleanse aforementioned sleeping bag, several tons of dry dog food, and her very own toothbrush.

--One phonograph, belonging to a teenager which, after playing "You Light Up My Life" 107 consecutive times, was inadvertently dropped out of a second floor window by the teenager's father.

--A bill from the gas company for $87.50, made necessary when a child's entire marble collection somehow found its way into the household heating ducts.

--An estimated 17,000 feathers, the natural by-product of a wrestling match between two siblings (and their pillows).

--An old green car which, although it is faithfully fed and watered by the adult members of this establishment, has developed the habit of absenting our driveway whenever we need it.

I could continue, dear IRS, but I'm sure you understand my plight. Just drop me a note stating which form I should use, and I promise faithfully not to fold, spindle, mutilate--or weep.

Miserably yours,
Mrs. A.

Dear God,

I've had another disagreement with my husband. He certainly has a temper, doesn't he? But then I've never been known for my placid, easygoing disposition.

Look at him, Father, sleeping so peacefully, as if the angry words which flashed between us had never taken place. How can he do that, Lord? Doesn't a guilty conscience ever torment him? Or has he learned to push it aside when more interesting possibilities present themselves? That's one trick I wish I could learn.

Here I pace, back and forth in the darkened house, filled with the small sounds of a family at rest. But there is no rest for me. Like a relentless recorder I replay the quarrel in my mind, thinking of things I wish I'd said, regretting the unkind remarks, wishing that we could communicate like two civil mature people ought to do. But he never listens, Father. And neither, quite often, do I.

I know that true listening requires a special skill, Lord. One must receive not only the spoken words, but also the meaning hidden underneath. It's difficult, Lord, for sometimes the truth is buried so deeply that touching is a hopeless task. But occasionally, a rare flash of insight occurs, a peek into the naked soul of the other--and I discover that he too is a weak trembling traveler, badly in need of my support on this lonely and confusing journey.

And that's what it's all about, isn't it Father? Two vulnerable people, masking their needs under a covering of angry accusations, each wanting to reveal his or her true self, but afraid of the rejection that so often comes. Somehow we have to keep trying, to stumble toward each other instead of turning away.

They say that a marriage has perished if there are no disagreements. If so, then ours must be truly flourishing! Help me to bring forth the positive, life-giving force that flows so steadily underneath our surface. Help me to respond to his needs, accept his weaknesses, and put aside the grudges that would be so easy to nurture. Help me to face tomorrow and the forgiveness I must offer.

And help me, Lord, once in awhile, to keep my big mouth shut.

Your loving child

Dear Patsy,

Your letter was a joy, but was it really necessary to enclose photos of the family cavorting in the California surf? Yes, I know you can't help the fact that west coast weather turns the rest of the country green with envy, but I really didn't need the reminder, old pal. Especially now.

You ask how our record-breaking winter has been, and just for that (and because I desperately need someone over three feet tall to talk to), I'll tell you.

--It's been coats--coats thrown everywhere, smelling of that wet-mold scent that spray bottles of detergent (or straight ammonia) will never banish. And boots left to drip in strategic locations--in the bathroom, on top of the furnace, underneath beds. And caps and scarves and only one mitten of a pair, trailing across the living room and into the hall. What fun we shall have tomorrow when our precious tykes search for their outside armor, cannot locate it, and fill the house with wails: "MO-ther! Where's my . . . ?" And MO-ther, resisting the impulse to set fire to everything woolen, will lock herself in a closet til the first thaw.

--It's been leaks, a steady beat-beat-beat of the tom-tom as we open our weary eyes each morning to discover yet another ceiling crack. "I refuse to sleep in this bed again until you do something about that water dripping over our heads!" I screamed at Spouse last Monday.

He did. He moved the bed.

--It's been garden hoses, hooked up to an inside water faucet, snaking their way across the dishwasher and out the kitchen exhaust fan. Hoses used by

Spouse, balanced precariously on a ladder and surrounded by clouds of steam, to melt the ice that's clogging the gutters that's causing the water to run inside the roof that's causing the beat-beat-beat. It's been wet clothes and a bout of pneumonia and a whopping doctor bill.

But the beat goes on . . .

--It's been endless shoveling, drifts so high that the kids look down on me through the windows. Gangs of boys leaping wildly off the garage roof, and falling three feet to the snow below. A natural toboggan slide in every yard. Shoveling until we finally get the driveway cleared (for the fourteenth time), and the city workers plow it shut again.

--It's been re-papertraining the dog, because if we let her out, she might vanish forever. And cars wearing red flags on their antennae so they will be noticed underneath the drifts. And weather reporters whose very appearance on the TV brings terror to your heart.

--It's been food, a budget-breaking supply dragged home to stem the boredom, a steady crackle of potato chip bags, and cookie baking, and crumbs covering every surface. And Mom stripping off her nail polish before daring to step on the scale.

--It's been snow days when the schools close and mothers weep and fathers take refuge in the basement. Endless Monopoly tournaments, phones that ring into the wee hours, shouts of "MO-ther, she stuck her tongue out at me!" followed by "Well, he's looking at me!" followed by MO-ther taking refuge in the basement.

--It's been the house going to pot and no one caring, because who wants to clean around the buckets in every room? And litter everywhere: trails of popcorn and scrap paper and dust balls and stale socks. And kids fingering golf clubs and tennis rackets and baseballs with longing written in their eyes. And a new houseplant, to remind oneself that green things still do grow--somewhere.

--It's been throwing a shoe at the TV as the weatherperson (whom I vowed this winter to desert) begins the forecast with ''Another six to eight inches expected tonight.'' And reading Chamber of Commerce literature from Florida, and counting the years to retirement.

--It's been ridiculous, unbelievable, laughable, and cryable. But we're still all together--healthy and warm--and I guess that's something to be very grateful for.

It will have to do, at least until I see the first crocus.

Enjoy your sunburn, Patsy. Good hearing from you.

Best,
Your pal

SPRING

Dear Diary,

Okay, go ahead and scold. I did promise to write to you on a regular basis, didn't I? But do you know how much correspondence is constantly piling up on my desk? (Why do so many people write to me?) And I still can't seem to find a pen (we have to keep the yellow crayons by the phone just in case a message must be taken for Husband).

As I slog through the puddles heralding this new season, I am feeling reborn, Diary, as if the memories of these past few months are simply the ravings of a demented mind, and life really begins only now. And yet, in a larger sense, perhaps I'm experiencing the end of an era, the finish of one segment of my existence, and am approaching a turn in life's road that will carry me in a new direction.

It happens to all of us, doesn't it? We live life the way we read a novel--becoming engrossed in a chapter, regretfully reaching the last page, then starting anew on the next episode. The story line, our situation in life, is fairly consistent, but the plot's sudden and unexpected twists and turns leave us surprised, angry, amused--but always eager for more.

And so it is with me. After an incredible number of years spent with my hands in a diaper pail, my cabinets stocked with strained spinach, I am approaching the end of an age. My youngest is no longer a baby. And sometime soon, the days will be mine again.

It is a passage, this new freedom, just as the early-married, new-mother, preschool-raiser, age-thirty episodes were all passages, new chapters to be read,

savored, shared, complained about--and then bid good-
bye. There is poignancy in each passage, but there is
hope, too, and eagerness, and a firm commitment to
see the book through to its conclusion, to discover how
it all will end.

And so my personal plot thickens. As I reclaim a
portion of my life, how shall it be spent? Pursuing a
career? Expanding my volunteer commitments? Going
back to school? Spending more time with friends? I
don't know yet. Only time will provide the answers I
seek.

It's difficult to say good-bye to a chapter of my life
that has been so rich, a phase that has forced me to
draw upon my deepest resources, to grow in spite of
myself.

But a new page is unfolding. And despite my hesitant
heart, it is time to say hello.

Love,
Me

Dear Mother Nature,

Spring is supposed to be such a nice season. It's the time of year when new life appears--tulips (if I remembered to plant the bulbs last fall), green-budded branches, and usually a nest or two of baby robins outside my kitchen window. And since you are in the midst of redecorating the outdoors, our neighborhood residents help you along as best we can. The dismal cold-weather grime is banished by crisp white paint on window frames, shiny waxed cars, and spruced-up garage interiors--all enlivening the landscape once again.

It's a sight for winter-weary eyes--if only I had time to look.

But I don't. Because when you made spring, Mother Nature, you also made it the busiest time of the year. And navigating our way through this annual turmoil requires the cool hand of a White House social secretary coupled with the physical constitution of a Grand Champion bull.

"Can you believe it?" my husband marveled one recent morning. "Three of our friends had babies this month. How did that happen?"

I shrugged. "In the usual way, I suppose."

"No, I mean how are we going to fit three christening parties into our schedule? It's bursting already."

I gave him a hopeful glance. "Maybe no one will invite us."

But we were whistling in the dark and we both knew it. When spring appears, can parties be far behind?

Or weddings, for that matter? I don't blame couples

for preferring to tie the knot under warm and sunny skies, but their marriages usually play havoc with mine.

"I think you ought to buy a new outfit for the Breen wedding," my husband told me yesterday. "Your 'going to a marriage' dress is getting awfully tacky."

"I know," I sighed. "Do you remember that guest at the Nelson wedding who told me, 'I don't remember your face, but your clothes are certainly familiar'?"

"Then again," my better half hesitated, "how can we afford your dress with all those crystal goblets and toasters to buy?"

I gave him a hopeful glance. "Maybe we could both get the flu?"

But it's wishful thinking, of course. There isn't time to be sick in the spring. After all, I must make a costume for my kindergartner who is to be Dancing Dewdrop in the forest sequence of her class play. Husband and I will attend the play, of course (and make spectacles out of ourselves by demanding an encore from Dancing Dewdrop), and will then stay on at school for the fifth-grader's band concert. We will discover midway through the first number that the fifth-grader is not on stage, because he left his trombone somewhere at home.

"How could anyone misplace a trombone?" Husband hisses at me during the intermission.

"I haven't cleaned the house in a month," I remind him. "It's spring, you know."

He knows. He knows because for the third year in a row he has signed up to coach Little League on Tuesday and Thursday evenings, which will conflict with my Tuesday night choir practice (we are rehearsing for Easter Services, the spring recital, and the Memorial Day parade, all at the same time). Coincidentally, Husband's sports schedule will also keep him from attending his Dancing Dewdrop's annual Indian Princess banquet.

"You did that on purpose!" I accused. "You know she's been looking forward to the dinner, and you deliberately found a way to get out of it!"

"I did not!" he defended himself. "Okay, so maybe I am getting tired of wearing that silly feather headdress and making beads out of old walnut shells. . . ."

"Indian Princesses is a very worthwhile activity," I remind him stiffly.

"Then you go to the dinner."

But I can't, of course. I have a conference scheduled with each of the children's teachers, the children all have appointments with their orthodontists, and I've scheduled an appointment at the vet's for the parakeet's toenail trim. There are spring wardrobes to be refurbished (the Indian Princess/Dancing Dewdrop is down to two left sneakers and a moccasin), sickly-looking plants to be repotted before they develop terminal root rot, two Mother's Day gifts to buy (three, if the kids forgot mine), and the dust balls under our bed seem to be permanently merging with the carpet. And worst of all, one of the kids is graduating from eighth grade.

"Let's see," I mused, looking at the school schedule. "You're supposed to learn 'We've Only Just Begun' by next Tuesday, and practice in your cap and gown on Thursday. . . ."

"I can't make it," Son mumbled around a pastrami-and-Swiss-cheese sandwich. "Those are Little League nights."

"Forget baseball," I told him. "Your father's dying to fill in for you, although your uniform is going to be a bit skimpy on him. And I suppose I ought to start a guest list for your party. . . ."

"All this fuss for a graduation," Son muttered in disgust.

I looked at him. And suddenly, beyond his freckled

face I saw another graduation, and another, and a wedding and a christening--all the landmarks of change and growth and the inevitable passage of time.

Soon, too soon, there will be quiet springs, easy languorous days in which to prune a rosebush, watch a cloud, listen to the sounds of a silent house. But the price of peace and solitude is much too high for me. Today there is a special kind of life, rolling and racing and rioting around me. Today it is the life I choose.

Thank you, Mother Nature, for this hectic--and oh so blessed--spring.

Sincerely,
The lady in the white house that needs painting

Dear Dr. Porter,

I'm never thrilled when you order me into the hospital for a short stay. It's hard work, you know, getting ready to be sick. One must break the news to one's husband--who will react with typical concern ("Good Lord! You mean I've got to take care of the kids?")--get the pile of clothes needing ironing into some sort of manageable dimensions, inventory the contents of refrigerator and cabinets, and prepare a "battle plan" to be followed when one is gone: "Roast on Monday, hash on Tuesday. Recipe for hash somewhere in third desk drawer. Soccer playoffs 2:15 Tuesday. Four year old to dentist 9 AM Wednesday--is not allowed to bring life-size panda or box of sweet cereal along on visit. Baby-sit for Jeffrey N. Wednesday afternoon, his mother switching nursery school duty with me. Can someone fix vacuum cleaner and/or washing machine while I'm gone?"

But the most intimidating part of a hospital procedure, at least to me, is the detailed explanation of what I will be going through, compliments of all those helpful souls who have already pulled their duty time in surgery, and are now eager to educate a neophyte.

"I hope you don't get that rotten tube down your throat," muses a woman from our choir's alto section.

"Just remember to cough a lot," recommends the check-out lady at my supermarket, "no matter how much it hurts."

"It'll be a snap," an encouraging friend reassures me. "Remember how fast I bounced back?" I remember, all right. She had a full-time housekeeper for three weeks afterwards and still couldn't stand up straight till Christmas.

Nevertheless, I square my shoulders, pack my suitcase, kiss the kids (most of whom must be dragged off the sandlot to say good-bye), and clutch my husband's hand as he drives me to my date with destiny. As usual, there are plenty of adjustments to be made.

What does one do, for instance, when one is a confirmed nicotine addict, and one's roommate turns pale at the sight of a match? Even worse, how shall I react if my roommate is in traction because she misread her copy of **Introduction to Yoga**, and insists on giving me a blow-by-blow account of her lawsuits against the publisher, the author, and the leotard manufacturer?

Is it against hospital rules to watch something other than game shows on daytime television? If a paramedic asks if he may "learn a little about IVs" by connecting mine, should I volunteer for the experiment? When a nurse mentions that she has terrible trouble deciphering my doctor's handwriting, is it considered bad form to weep quietly? And why, Dr. Porter, if I blink my eyes, will I miss your daily visit?

After a few days, however, things look a bit brighter, and the telephone brings cheerful messages from the outside world.

"Mom," pleads the fourteen year old, "how soon are you coming home?"

"Why? Isn't Dad taking care of things?"

"He sure is. Just like Captain Queeg."

A neighbor phones in a report on the latest shopping center episode. "Your husband reacted splendidly when your daughter got away from him--just dashed right into the traffic and grabbed her. Of course, a lot of the eggs broke when the shopping cart tipped over, but . . . ."

My husband takes it all in stride. "Everything's

under control," he advises me at visiting time, "especially now that all the kids are sleeping in the garage. How soon are you coming home?"

Good question. Despite the staff's kind attention, my roommate and I are so bored that we have begun building castles out of bedpans, thermometers, and old coffee cups. The kitchen crew has cut off our lunchtime wine, and even the Candy Stripers refuse to deliver our flowers. The day that an intern inadvertently backs into my nail file, I am officially discharged.

The neighborhood looks so different as we drive home, and I am overwhelmed by the pots of mums, homemade soup, and cookies sent over by dear Grandma and our loving friends. Husband has managed to paint the bedroom and claims that the plumber says definitely that he will unplug the upstairs bathroom toilet tomorrow. The house is standing, the kids are sitting, Husband is smiling--and my cup is running over.

Especially when an old friend phones to welcome me home and confides that she will be entering the hospital next week for surgery. "It will work out fine, Irene," I assure her in my most professional manner. "Just do what the doctors tell you, and remember to cough a lot." And then, because I simply cannot resist it, I offer her one more word of advice. "Irene, dear, I do hope you don't get that rotten tube down your throat."

After all, what are friends for?

See you in Ward B!

Sincerely,
Mrs. A.

April 4

Dear Author,

I found your book **What to Do with a Three Year Old on a Rainy Day** quite interesting. (And judging from the fact that my three year old ate the cover of the book, I would assume that he, too, enjoyed it.) There are just a few minor problems that I would like to call to your attention.

In the chapter, "Let's Make a Rhythm Band," I was quite taken with the many different instruments that can be constructed from simple household gadgets. I had no trouble assembling a comb kazoo, a pie pan tambourine (although sewing coat buttons onto aluminum foil proved somewhat time-consuming--said three year old took apart my grandfather clock while I was making the attempt), or even a shoe-box-and-rubber-band banjo. But frankly, your Humming Flute is all wet, and I mean that literally. Have you ever given a paper towel tube to a preschooler and told him to simply sing into it? It's much more creative from his point of view to suck on it/look through it/beat a neighbor over the head with it. Which brings me to another problem I encountered: it seemed such a shame to waste all these ingenious musical items on just one child, so I ended up inviting all the other three year olds on the block over for a concert. Which helped their mothers pass the rainy afternoon very well, but didn't do much for me.

The sock-puppet section was quite clever. We already had several fingerless gloves and toeless socks in our domain, so gathering them together for an impromptu show was no problem. However, I found your decorating-the-puppet instructions rather impractical. I did, of course, use "yarn and/or popsicle sticks" as you suggested. But I might remind you that the average household does not include "pink sequins, blue rubber balls (one-inch diameter), or miniature natural-hair wigs." By the time I had rounded up all this paraphernalia from the neighbors, my three year old had stuffed up the downstairs toilet with the aforementioned fingerless gloves and toeless socks. Which made our rainy day interesting (he absolutely adores Al the plumber), but also rather expensive.

Frankly, the milk carton blocks were a delight (although I do think the instructions should have reminded Mother to remove the milk first), and so was the Throw the Penny into the Box game (although ours ended up between the piano keys, on top of the light fixture, and upstairs). But I have some reservations about your Bubbles in the Sink section. It went over well, but your blithe directions to "wipe up puddles on floor" might more honestly read, "Build an ark for remaining family members."

Since your book is selling well, I have an idea for a sequel. Next time, why don't you consider **What to Do with a Mother on a Rainy Day**? Suggestions might include mother reading a novel, talking uninterrupted on the phone, or taking a nap--while other family members play The Lint Hunt (participants gather small fragments of dirt or dust from carpet and deposit them in nearest trash container); the Pick-Up-Your-Room Challenge (participants see who can be first to clear a path from bedroom door to bedroom window); or the Fix-a-Dinner Game (participants race to set table and cook nourishing meal as a surprise for napping mother). Now there would be a real best-seller!

Happy writing!
Mrs. A.

April 9

Dear Mrs. Champaign,

Your efficiency is mind-boggling--what would I do without you? Even more interesting--what would all the students (last-name letters A through GR) who depend on you for everything from deciphering a computerized report card to giving clear directions to the archery court to sorting out conflicts with the history teacher--do without you?

Being a high school guidance counselor calls for patience, a strong stomach, and nerves of cast iron (just the sight of all that hair, on a daily basis, would certainly make my teeth tingle). And I'll bet you receive very few accolades for your perseverance. Therefore, please allow me to bestow a much-deserved pat on your back. Thanks to you, our eldest son is well on his way to making an intelligent college choice.

I must admit that the first book you sent home, **Do You Need College--Even More Appropriate, Does College Need You**? had me up till the wee hours for several nights in a row. I really had no idea how many institutions of higher learning abound in our land. Everything from "Ed's U.--Welding Our Specialty" to the Hallowed Halls of Harvard was listed, and seemed to have something to recommend it. My first task, obviously, was to prod Son by process of elimination into deciding just what sort of education he was after.

Since Son is interested in hotel and restaurant management, in addition to space exploration and, quite possibly, Philosophies of the Third World, we had rather interesting dialogues in attempting to decide on a course of study. (The neighbors will recount to you just how interesting.) Eventually, however, Son narrowed his choices, which allowed us to dispose of several hundred universities as well (not literally, you understand).

At this point we were able to take a closer look at incidentals such as size and location, and we discovered that Son had some definite preferences along these lines. For example, he is ruling out institutions with more than ten thousand students because he will not receive enough attention. He is ruling out institutions with less than one thousand students because he will be noticed a bit too much. Any school in the running must provide an 18-hole golf course within its campus boundaries, the greens fees preferably included in tuition costs. If the school offers female golfers as well, it goes automatically to the top of the list.

Mother has some preferences, too; the university must be located on a bus or train line linked directly to our front door, to avoid constant grumblings when Father must take to the highway to pick up or deliver Son and assorted goods. The school must have, in its bylaws, a firm rule against shipping dirty laundry home. It must maintain strict weekend curfews (9 PM sounds about right), and must sturdily support leisure activities such as square dancing and taffy pulls. Only the faculty may drive cars (and then, only if they are over thirty).

Because of this helpful book of yours, Mrs. Champaign, Son and I, putting together our demands, were able to eliminate several more schools, leaving only about 1500 on a roster of possibilities. It was then that you thoughtfully sent home a listing of tuition, board and room costs, and miscellaneous fees for the above-mentioned institutions, allowing us to prune a bit further. We are now down to six schools.

We have discovered, thanks to your inclusion of Forms FAR, WH-2, and R2D2, that Son must choose a school within our state borders if he wishes to receive any state aid. Of course, since he may not discover whether he qualifies for state aid until the precise moment he is unpacking his gym shorts and meeting his roommate, such a procedure seems slightly risky. Nonetheless, I have gone ahead and filed the forms, with the exception of WH-2 which, if I interpret the small print correctly, cannot be mailed until after June 1st or upon our receiving Japanese citizenship, whichever comes first.

I have also inspected the list of possible scholarship offers, but since I am not a member of the Daughters of the American Revolution, Son is (unfortunately) prosaicly brown-eyed and right-handed, and my husband recently resigned from his bowling league, it seems we will not be receiving any honoraria. Son will, of course, work while on campus, but since he cannot apply for a job (Form 39-L) until after admission, and may not be admitted until we get the results from Forms FAR and R2D2 (see above), we find ourselves in a rather peculiar situation.

However, with typical bravery, Son is now applying to two of these schools. He has filled out the four-page applications and will be bringing them to your office today. Would you mind digging out transcripts of his grades, copies (in triplicate) of his standardized test scores, and filling out (with #2 lead pencil) the guidance counselor's report which must accompany each application. I would be most grateful for your help.

Isn't it fortunate that you have only another few hundred of these to do before the end of the term? Otherwise, you might become overworked. . . .

Gratefully,
Chris's Mom

Tip Toe Tulips, Inc.

Gentlemen:

We are now well into the spring season, and the bulbs I ordered from you and planted last fall are certainly brightening our front yard. In fact, they're brightening it just a bit too dramatically. Even our mailman is wearing sunglasses.

You see, I distinctly remember ordering yellow and white bulbs, and I swear the packages were marked that way, too. I planted the yellows around our house's foundation--they were supposed to echo (smartly) our yellow awnings and provide a spot of color in front of those plain green bushes. The white tulips were intended to border our new purple plum tree.

Imagine my surprise (and my husband's language) when the yellow tulips turned out to be red and white, and the poor plum tree got bordered in orange. Frankly, it isn't what I had in mind.

Complicating the situation are the pink-and-blue crocuses I forgot about last year. They seem somehow to have moved across the yard and are popping up in the most unlikely places--along the sidewalk, under the fence and, of course, much too near our bewildered plum tree. I realize that the crocuses are not your problem, but perhaps you ought to have a talk with the fellows in your shipping department. Hopefully, they could choose another way to liven up their working day? (Or maybe I need new reading glasses.)

Sincerely,
A Disgruntled Consumer

Newton's Nursery

Gentlemen:

Last fall my husband purchased a plum tree from your establishment for our front lawn. Dutifully, he dug the required eighteen-inch hole, added fertilizer, mulched with peat moss, and talked to the plum tree each night for a week

You were right--the tree is now thriving. Which is unfortunate, because we find we must move it to the other side of the yard. Can you give us any pointers on safe transplanting? Or perhaps you know of a place that dyes awnings?

Sincerely,
A Hopeful Consumer

Dear Husband

Okay, so the neighbors are pointing and laughing, and Newton's Nursery refuses to accept any responsibility if we so much as breathe in the tree's direction. We've never pretended to be professional landscape artists. Where's your sense of humor?

I've rejected your solution, that of using all the tulips as fuel for our Memorial Day barbeque. And you've rejected mine (I suppose a stockade fence would be too expensive). The only alternative, I guess, is to wait for summer and a new crop of flowers, hopefully color coordinated this time.

By the way, you weren't planning to put those tomato plants along the backyard fence, were you? I've already planted strawberries there. I think.

Love,
Me

Dear Kathy,

Thank you, thank you for the very special coffee klatching at your house yesterday. It's always fun to get away from my kitchen (even just to visit the laundry room), but I think our group has something special, don't you?

Perhaps it's the easy way we can converse on any subject. Just hand us a topic and we're off and running--each woman bringing her own unique viewpoint to the conversation. How often we've discussed (and disagreed on) church renewal, potty training, the latest hemline, the state of the union--all of us contributing our own colors to this riotous palette of diversity.

To differ, and yet remain loved--perhaps this is our strength. Each of us is very much her own person, yet all fit together like pieces of a golden mosaic. If one member is missing, we all become a bit poorer.

Perhaps the sharing is what binds us together in these very special moments. We are not afraid to let our masks slip, to appear as we really are--sometimes confused, vulnerable, lonely, sometimes on top of the world. There need be no fear of self-discovery, no hiding from truths too difficult to acknowledge. The group is there, accepting, trusting, wrapping each woman in a warm cocoon of laughter, tenderness, and love.

I leave each coffee klatch in a state of refreshed bliss, and the glow lingers as I rejoin my family, begin my household rounds once more. There is a rhythm to my labors, a rejuvenation of my spirit which carries me through the ordinary tasks, and makes them--and me--

somehow more satisfying. For a little while I have
touched another, and she has spoken to me with words
of the heart. For a little while, the treasure of
communication has been mine.

God so loved the world that he sent us friends to
reflect his infinite beauty in their eyes.

Thank you, Kathy, for yesterday.

Love,
Joan

Dear Jesus,

Today we commemorate your death. It is the saddest and most profound day in all the year, this Good Friday. How I long to share it with you, watching three hours in the quiet darkness of my church.

But my witness must take a different path, Jesus. Here in my kitchen there are lunches to be made, a baby needing clean diapers, a thousand details needing my attention. I cannot watch with you.

Not for me, the peaceful call of quiet meditation. I go a different direction--polishing shoes for tonight's service, taking telephone messages for a working husband, chasing a toddler up the stairs. Not for me, the silent contemplation. I must prepare supper, wash just one more load of clothes, one more pair of sticky hands.

Don't be disappointed in me, Jesus. As you gaze upon me from your cross of suffering, know that I am lifting my heart to you. Although my crosses are tiny, they divert me, burden me, keep me from appreciating your sacrifice to the fullest. And yet this is where you want me to be, here within this family that you and I have made.

There will be other Good Fridays when the pace has slackened, the children matured. Once more I will visit you as I did in those carefree days long ago. But today, Jesus, I offer you only an orderly house, a hurried prayer, a faraway glance at Golgotha. May my small gift console you ever so slightly as we wait together for the joy of Resurrection.

Your child

April 22

9:15 AM

Tim--Dentist appointment has been changed from four
to three PM today. REMEMBER! Brush your teeth
before you go.

9:30 AM

Chris--Kathy from the hamburger stand called. Wants
to know if you will work the Saturday night shift for
her, but only if she can sub for you this Friday from
5 to 9 PM.
If Friday is out, please call her back at the stand
between three and six today, or see her tomorrow in
history class. If Friday is okay, then ignore her in
history class, except if you can work until 10 PM, in
which case you should slip her a note.
Kathy also wishes to know if she left her lipstick in
your car yesterday.
Yours truly would also like an answer to that
question.

10:15 AM

Billy--You left your putter over at Jeff's house. Please
run over to his house right away and pick it up as
his mother is arranging a garage sale. If you would
like for her to sell the putter, do not respond to this
message.

10:40 AM

Nancy, Honey--A little girl just called about a birthday party this afternoon. Did you forget to tell Mommy something, Sweetheart?

11:02 AM

Husband--A Mr. Fowler phoned--has been trying to get through since 9:15 this morning. I explained that I am merely a domestic employee here, and that the household members are all enjoying a day off, but he sounded quite irritated anyway. Call him back right away.

11:31 AM

Billy--You left your second baseman's mitt on the ball diamond at the park. Mr. Henry found it and says you may pick it up at the Lost and Found between three and seven PM anytime this week. Now aren't you glad Mom insisted on those stick-on identification tags? (Maybe you ought to wear one on your nose.)

12:15 PM

Tim--Bowling team practice will be an hour earlier than usual tonight. If you cannot make it, call Bud after 3 PM today. By the way, you'll be in the dentist chair at 3 PM--REMEMBER your appointment!

12:40 PM

Husband--Haven't you called Mr. Fowler back yet?
Quite excitable, isn't he? I'm leaving to drive Nancy
to a birthday party--back by one. I think it's
important that you call Mr. Fowler.

12:45 PM

MOM--AUNT SUE CALLED. CALL HER BACK. I
THINK SHE HAD THE BABY. GOT MESSAGES. IF
KATHY CALLS, TELL HER YES. GOING BOWLING--
CHRIS

12:50 PM

MOM--MRS. SERB CALLED. ARE WE GOING
THERE SATURDAY NIGHT? IF SO, BRING THE
POTATO SALAD RECIPE. OR MAYBE THE POTATO
SALAD. SOME MAN CALLED FOR DAD. GOT
MESSAGES. WILL NOT FORGET DENTIST. HAD A
PIECE OF THE CHOCOLATE CAKE. OK? PLAYING
TENNIS--TIM

12:55 PM

MOM--SOME EDITOR FROM NEW YORK CALLED.
SOUNDED EXCITED. SAID IT WAS IMPORTANT.
CALL HER RIGHT BACK. FORGOT TO GET NAME
OR NUMBER. HOW COME I NEVER GET ANY
PHONE MESSAGES?--BRIAN

1:20 PM

Billy--You left your Monopoly game at baby-sitting job
last night. Boardwalk and Marvin Gardens totally
annihilated by Mrs. Fisher's children. Requests pickup while Chance cards still intact. You also left your
math book there.
Brian--You have FIVE MINUTES to remember that
editor's name!

1:40 PM

Chris--Call Mike about experiment for science due
Monday. Something about digging for earthworms
under a full moon?
Tim--It was not okay to eat the chocolate cake. It was
for the Serb's party.

2:10 PM

Husband--Call office about Mr. Fowler. Has lodged
complaint with your boss, and also with telephone
company.

2:45 PM

Chris--Kathy called again and said to disregard entire
original message. She found a substitute for her shift
and has also located her lipstick. (Why would she
ever think she left her lipstick in your car? Kindly
see me after supper.)

3:18 PM

Tim--Good show, sport. You forgot your dentist
  appointment. Call office and reschedule. And don't
  talk to me for at least an hour.

4:10 PM

Brian--A phone message at last! Your dog is over on
  State road at the fire station. Pick her up before we
  get a citation. Thanks for finally remembering that
  editor's name. I returned her call but she had
  already left for the day.

4:15 PM

Husband--Tonight's Cub Scout car pool has been
  rerouted. You pick up Kenny first, since the rest of
  his family will be gone by 7:30 and he obviously
  shouldn't be alone in an empty house. (I know he
  lives on the other side of town, but as you're
  doubling back, you can stop for Greg and Matthew.)
  Peter will be sleeping over at Mike's house, so you
  can skip his stop. And David's mother will deliver
  him to the meeting, since his trampoline lesson will
  be running late tonight.
  Also, don't forget to pick up some potato chips,
  pretzels, and cola on the way--it's our turn to supply
  the goodies.
  And while you're at the store, will you pick up some
  pretzels for me?
  By the way, who is Mr. Fowler and what was he
  calling you about?

4:40 PM

Billy--Did you bring home wrong gym shorts? Check
   laundry basket and phone coach.

5:00 PM

Attention, all members of this household: Your
   telephone answering service is going off duty, and is
   planning to soak her ear in a nice warm bubble bath.
   Henceforth, all ting-a-lings shall be either ignored, or
   handled by someone whose lips are still functioning.
   It's been a long day. . . .
Husband--When you get the pretzels, will you bring
   home dinner, too?

April 26

Dear Aunt Emily,

Yes, the family rumor is true--I am now the proud owner of a real honest-to-goodness car of my own. With two teenagers who had each earned an A in Driver's Education (plus yours truly who was getting awfully tired of going back and forth to the store on roller skates), it was inevitable that our family would eventually add a car. In fact, the only member who was not ecstatic about our decision was the Head of the House. "Gasoline costs money," he pronounced sagely, with the assurance of one who will drive to the corner mailbox rather than risk wearing out the soles of his twenty-year-old work boots.

"But we'll be using the car only in times of dire need," I pointed out. "Like getting the boys to work, hitting the underwear sale at Sears, racing a pneumonia victim to the hospital, my Tuesday night bridge club. . . ."

"I see," Husband nodded seriously. "Just bona fide emergencies. . . ."

"Exactly."

And so, sometime later, an ancient green sedan, christened Betsy, became a member of our family. Battle-scarred and rusted, she wore her dents proudly and, at least at first, delivered us to our destinations in a trustworthy manner. But when the flu season hit, and she developed a cough more raucous than any of our offspring's, I decided rather belatedly that perhaps she needed a checkup too.

Betsy was admitted to the nearest auto hospital for tests, and it was almost two days before the mechanic summoned up enough courage to call me in for a consultation. He was obviously in a state of extreme agitation, and I tried my best to put him at ease.

"Just give it to me straight, Al," I told him staunchly. "What's wrong with Betsy?"

"Well," he swallowed convulsively, "have you noticed that when you apply the brakes, Betsy immediately swerves into the opposite lane?"

"Of course," I reassured him. "That's why I humor her by staying under fifteen miles an hour."

"And do you think," he went on, somewhat glassy-eyed, "that the steering seems a bit loose?"

"The wheel revolves four or five times for each turn," I pointed out proudly. "Not many cars can match that record!"

"And one of the back tires isn't touching the ground anymore," Al sighed gloomily.

I leaned forward earnestly. "Can Betsy be saved, Al?"

"I'll do my level best," he promised, "but you'd better look into a second mortgage or a full-time job."

I shrugged. "Where can you get a car in good running order these days for a paltry $469.70?"

Betsy was worth every penny of our overextended budget, and shortly after being released from intensive care, she rewarded my faith by once again transporting us around town, her little engine humming happily. At least that's what my husband and sons told me. I was allowed to use the car only between the hours of 2 and 6 AM on Wednesdays and Fridays, which made it rather difficult for me to appreciate Betsy's $469.70 purr.

"Look," I tried to explain to Spouse one morning, "Betsy is supposed to be my car, and I'm planning to claim her on Form 1040 as a dependent. Why, therefore, do you have to drive her on all these little errands?"

"It's easier than taking the plastic wrap off of my

car," he explained. "And besides, you have Betsy most of the day. . . ."

"Oh, really?" I answered sarcastically. "For your information, I haven't seen Betsy since last Thursday. If the boys aren't taking her to the movies, then it's baseball practice, or . . . ."

"The boys?" he interrupted, stunned. "Do they still live here?"

"Who do you think just passed us on a five-minute pit stop?"

"You mean, that large person who grabbed the leftover leg of lamb and your gasoline credit card was . . . ."

I nodded solemnly. "Our eldest."

By putting the teens up for adoption, I eventually reclaimed Betsy, and during the next several months she made many new friends for our family. As I'd chug past Sam's E-Z Drive, he would wave and yell, "Need a tow today, Mrs. A?" When I filled up at the corner station, the attendants (all, by now, on a first-name basis) would pat Betsy's fender affectionately, and inquire after her carburetor. And when a neighborhood teen mechanic discovered that I had had new tires put on, his concern was really touching. "You didn't," he kept murmuring and shaking his head. "Tell me you didn't . . ."

I shrugged. "Where can you get a car in good running order for a paltry $219.50?"

Eventually, however, our final crisis came. Betsy's transmission failed, and she would chug only forward, but not in reverse. "We could put in a circular driveway," I suggested to Husband. "That way, I wouldn't have to back up whenever I run away from home . . ."

"Out of the question," he snapped.

"But where can you get a car in good running order for a paltry $1162.47?" I asked.

"Plenty of places," he told me, "and I suggest you start looking--now!"

We left Betsy at a nearby auto graveyard. Our six year old played taps on her kazoo, but the gesture didn't banish my tears. Even the dealer's promise to bury Betsy under a headstone shaped like a lemon left me unmoved. Silently, I turned away and headed for the exit, stopping only as we passed a small red convertible sagging inconspicuously in a corner of the car lot. I stared at her as the kids surrounded me. "She has a certain dignity, doesn't she?" I murmured.

"I'll say!" the eighth grader enthused. "No windshield to get dirty, and that chartreuse door really adds a touch of class."

"And look, Mommy!" added the six year old. "Her headlights keep winking off and on. Isn't that cute?"

After all, as I told Spouse later, where can you get a car in good running order these days for only $15.95?

You'll have to come over and meet her, Aunt Emily!

Love,
Your niece

May 1

Dear New Neighbors,

Welcome to our humble street! You will notice that
none of us has called upon you as of yet, and none of
us intends to--at least not until after your living room
drapes have gone up, or your son breaks one of our
windows, whichever comes first. We aren't unfriendly;
it's just that, having gone through it ourselves, we
realize that new families need a chance to settle in,
before being bombarded by visitors.

You will meet (or at least hear) our children, of
course, long before you lay eyes on any of us. This is
inevitable since just within the four houses directly
across the street there reside nine teenagers, eleven
grade school kids and four noisy toddlers--most of
them male. (Which is why only one question will be
asked of you during the coming weeks--"Do you have
any daughters?" We like to keep the neighborhood
ecology in balance.)

You will notice that our block is a pleasant mingling
of senior citizens, young couples, tiny starter homes
and enviable "custom-builts." The diversity suits us
all, since the neighborhood provides at least three
friends per age group. Families have been known to
start married life at the end of the street, buy a
residence six houses down when the third baby comes
along, remove a dormer or two as the kids start high
school, and eventually retire to the two-bedroom ranch
at the corner. As you can see, we are loyal to each
other.

We probably live so harmoniously because by tacit
agreement, we abide by a set of block rules. As
Chairperson of the Welcoming Committee, therefore, I

have taken the liberty of slipping the enclosed bylaws into your mailbox. Any questions should be directed to our Block Captain (the haggard-looking father of eight who sleeps in that rather spiffy-looking yellow tent).

1. If someone wishes to pass an uninterrupted year or two revarnishing her woodwork in peace, such activities shall be respected. If it has been "one of those days" however, and she is desperate for the sight and sound of another adult, the accepted signal is to sit forlornly on her front stoop for a moment or two; all strolling neighbors will then stop to chat.

2. Raucous outdoor parties are perfectly acceptable, provided the host also invites those living directly east, west, north, and south of his amplifier.

3. Happy parents usually announce the arrival of a new offspring by hanging the appropriately-colored bow on their front door. When the bow is taken down, phone calls and oglers are welcome.

4. All children will be permitted to swim in all backyard pools at all times--provided their mothers come along to supervise.

5. If someone inherits half a million dollars, it is considered poor taste to erect a moat around one's property or keep a champion race horse in the garage. Under these circumstances, one is expected to either continue wringing his hands over the newly-enacted sewer tax, or move to a classier neighborhood.

6. All community sand discovered in the hair or socks of a child at bath time automatically becomes the property of the finder.

7. Once a year, a combination block party/garage sale will be held, for the express purpose of discovering where everyone's missing tools have ended up. Music for this event will be provided by the three teenage tuba players living in the yellow bungalow.

8. Volkswagens should not be left at the curb on garbage pickup days.

9. Fred the mailman asks that we refrain from snappy comments about his Bermuda shorts. (Or the fact that he will deliver fourth-class mail only every second Tuesday.)

10. If a washing machine repair vehicle is sighted anywhere in the vicinity, all housewives will form a human barricade around said vehicle, refusing to move until the mechanic agrees to check all the other machines in the neighborhood which have been waiting for a service call since last Christmas.

In addition, we'd like you to know that the library is only six blocks away, all dogs should be leashed (except when they are playing second base), milk delivery is on Thursday, the daily paper is always late (and don't complain to the paperboy's mother--she lives next door to you), the best dill pickle buy is at the little grocery store in town, and there's a nest of new bunnies in your front hedges.

Happy to have you aboard, neighbors! I'll be by shortly to collect for the new sod we are buying to repair the parkway. (It's so exciting to have a real drag-racing champion living on this very street, isn't it?)

Sincerely,
The Lady in the House
with the Multi-colored Front Yard

Dear Mom,

For your unwavering trust in me through all our years together . . .

For opening the doors of the world to me, helping me develop my talents, recognizing my potential, arming me with principles that could last a lifetime . . .

For building a secure and peaceful home, where love echoed in every room . . .

For giving me a shoulder to cry on, and a sense of humor more precious because it was shared . . .

For warmly accepting the extended family I brought to you, and making each member feel valued and unique . . .

For your wisdom and advice, offered only when requested (and for all the times you bit your tongue) . . .

For being the perfect role model, secure in your own identity, yet always willing to change and grow . . .

For admitting often that you weren't perfect (and never expecting me to be) . . .

For taking the time to listen and share,

For letting me know that you really care,

But most of all, just for BEING THERE . . . .

. . . I love you.

Happy Mother's Day.

Your daughter

May 10

Dear Sis,

So my nephew has reached the magic age of twelve--
and you'd like some survival tips? I'll do my best, pal,
but as you are learning, Twelve is a most perplexing
age.

Twelve is a child of contradictions, suddenly taking
four showers a day (last year we had to introduce him
to a bar of soap) and flying into a panic if his hair
hasn't been shampooed since morning. But his
bedroom is a veritable sty, with dirty socks in various
stages of rigor mortis and last week's stale jeans mixed
in with the balled-up sheets and blankets. His feminine
counterpart doesn't make sense either. Her closet is
packed tightly with garments but, according to her,
she has "nothing to wear."

Remember those cozy mother-daughter chats, cookie-
baking sessions, shopping trips, Brownie meetings?
They're gone. The female Twelve is now in a period of
chronic humiliation, the cause of which is apparently
her mother. This parent, who was adored and imitated
by a younger daughter, is now a constant source of
embarrassment to this same child, suddenly turned
preteen. Cries of "Oh, Mother-r-r, you just don't
understand!" ring through a previously peaceful
household (accompanied by the now-familiar racing-up-
the-stairs-and-slamming-the-door routine). Mom's
clothes are old-fashioned, her hairstyle dated, her
attitude feudal, and her mere existence a problem. It
does little good to reassure Mom that by the time her
daughter is seventeen, Mom will have to keep her
clothing and makeup under lock and key and buy
earplugs for relief from Daughter's incessant chatter.

What counts, unfortunately, is today, and how to stay sane with a Twelve in residence.

A preteen son, while less vocally dramatic or critical, is just as irritating. He now scorns his father's invitation--"How 'bout going for a milkshake, Sport?" (After all, what if the gang saw him out in public with his father?)--and wouldn't be caught dead carrying on a conversation with anyone older than eighteen. While he'll burn up the telephone lines talking with his peers, he develops a startling reticence around the house. "Huh?" "Who, me?" and "Pass the potatoes" is about as chummy as he gets. It falls to Mom to explain to younger siblings that Twelve's "you, dummy!" is actually a term of endearment.

Twelve is a materialistic age--never again will the correct label on a pair of sneakers be so significant. Our preteens keep the national economy humming with their absolute need for stereos (and appropriate albums to be played at ear-splitting decibals), a complete wardrobe update at six-month intervals, and fashionable sports equipment. When parents suggest that their offspring earn the cash for these goodies, Twelve is apt to go into cardiac arrest (or shift into the classic run-upstairs-slam-door scene). According to Twelve's viewpoint, Mom and Dad owe him not only love, food, shelter, clothing, schooling, movie tickets, orthodontia, immunizations, contact lenses, and music lessons but also an annual vacation in Florida, personal taxi service, a home chemistry lab, and the latest in designer jeans.

What inexperienced parents are just beginning to learn about Twelve has been recognized for years by the educational system. That's why most preteens are quarantined from the rest of civilization and herded into junior-high buildings where, hopefully, their obnoxious behavior will not infect the remaining student population. Here, in a domain all their own, junior-high kids pursue the same puzzling behavior--spending their days shrieking and giggling, explaining why they didn't have time to do their homework, eating pizza for lunch, complaining about science class, pasting photos of rock stars on their lockers, and commiserating about the discipline at home. Junior-high teachers are easily recognized at PTA functions--their eyes are slightly glazed, they wear hearing aids, have a peculiarly hysterical laugh, and always maintain loudly that they LOVE teaching sixth and seventh grade.

It's no surprise that a Twelve is barely tolerated in his neighborhood. It is he who is still trick-or-treating at 10 PM on Halloween. It is she who will play lovingly with the younger kids on Tuesday, then refer to them disparagingly as "babies!" on Thursday. Fortunately, most households have either lived through a Twelve or are going to be doing it someday, so parents sigh in exasperation or look the other way.

Twelve can be a brutal experience, and perhaps the one hardest hit is the child. Being Twelve is an emotional roller-coaster ride, with newly-emerging hormones whirling in unpredictable patterns. No longer a child, yet not ready for adulthood, feet suddenly too large and feelings too shaky, testing authority yet needing security as never before--Twelves are vulnerable, uncertain, and perplexed. Eventually the skies will clear, and a calmer, surer, more delightful person will emerge from the turbulence, someone who will be our pal forever.

But what can we do with our Terrible Twelves in the meantime? Stand firm, be reassured, pray a lot--and love them.

You can do it, Sis! Hang in there!

Love,
The Voice of Experience

Dear Family,

Does anyone know where I can get a bigger kitchen calendar--preferably one covering the entire west wall? If not, someone is going to have to order me a set of bifocals or a huge magnifying glass. This situation is getting out of hand.

Personally, I don't see why you kids can't put your appointments on your own calendars, instead of cluttering up my kitchen log. And such microscopic entries, too! It wasn't until I got to the dentist's reception room today that I discovered that "MOM - 2 D" referred to the high school's Month of Math exhibit at which Second Son is giving a demonstration on the Integration of the Natural Logarithm of the Binomial Function to the Kth Power. Fine for you guys, but all I've got to show for the mistake is a filling in my twelve-year molar and a parking ticket.

I also don't see why you, Mr. Fourth Grader, find it necessary to record every social obligation that may conceivably come your way. For instance, on Monday of this week you have duly noted, "Jimmy comes over"; on Tuesday, "I go to Jimmy's"; and on Wednesday, "Fight with Jimmy, go to Ingrid's." Thursday reminds us that "Jimmy comes over," and on Friday you are to "Feed fish, empty wastebaskets, go to Jimmy's." Such notations take up valuable calendar space and are best recorded in a diary or chore chart. By the way, dear one, who's Ingrid?

Things get especially difficult when every member of the family has something to do on the same day. I call your attention to the 21st of this month (at least, I think it's the 21st--it's hard to read under all that scribbling). On this auspicious occasion, someone in our family is attending: a golf tournament (bring both putters); a hair-cutting session; tryouts for the eighth-grade trampoline squad; a job interview at Patrick's Pizzeria (bring Social Security card and proof of Italian heritage); a preschool birthday party; and a trombone lesson. I notice that our expectant gerbil is also due at the vet's for an iron shot, and that the 21st is the deadline for my room-mother phone calls for the PTA potluck supper. You can see my dilemma, of course. There's no room left on the calendar for the nervous breakdown I was planning to schedule.

As for those of you who keep suggesting that we use a school calendar with events already printed for each month, may I respectfully remind you that our family's students attend three schools, not to mention Adult Ed., and I have no desire to cross-check three different listings before making appointments for my ingrown toenail surgery.

Yesterday I went hunting for kitchen wallpaper bearing a calendar motif. I figured we could all just reach across the breakfast table and jot down our commitments, then replace the paper when we worked our way over to the refrigerator. But I'm having second thoughts on this, gang. For one thing, I've grown rather fond of the jelly spatters permanently etched on the wall behind the high chair, and would hate to see them go. For another, could we stand to look at each other's handwriting at breakfast, lunch, and dinner? Don't forget--we're the family who, by popular demand, is required to use a typewriter for all checks, notes, and school assignments.

And while we're on the subject of chicken scrawls, can someone please decipher the entry written for the third of next month? As I read it, we are either invited to a picnic that day, or our mortgage is going to be foreclosed.

I admit I've reached a dead end on this problem, gang, and no reasonable suggestions will be ignored. Just write them on the calendar, where I'll be sure to see them.

Love,
Mom

May 25

To My Eighth-Grade Graduate--

Tomorrow is a special day for you--another of the many milestones that must mark your passage from childhood into adult life. Together your father and I will watch as you march proudly down the aisle, and wonder, as we have wondered so often through the years, "Where did the time go?"

The banquet committee asked for a baby picture of you to hang alongside your cap-and-gown portrait. So I sent one of my favorites, a snapshot of you at six months, clutching your beloved stuffed rabbit, both of you grinning toothlessly into the camera. How many years stretched before you then--endless summer mornings to investigate a lazy backyard bumblebee, or splash in a blue wading pool surrounded by rubber duckies and cheerful plastic pails. Long winter afternoons, Old Maid tournaments, and rock collections spread under the dining room table. Life was limitless then, I thought. The bubbly package of energy and affection who had completely stolen my heart would remain forever small, forever innocent. But it was not so.

For graduation brings you one step closer to the final "good-bye," one pace farther along the road to maturity, wisdom, and separation from those who love you more than anyone could. "We've Only Just Begun," your class will sing tomorrow at this most important and hope-laden assembly. And yet for us, your parents, the job is nearly over.

We are proud, of course. Proud of your labor, your dedication, your sacrifices through the years which have led to tomorrow's academic triumph. "Promoted to high school," stamped so impressively on your last report card, represents far more than words. You alone know how many hours of evening study, book reports, research papers, and exams have earned this coveted and well-deserved diploma.

But even more important, we are proud of you as a person. The compassion, integrity, and clear thinking that emerges from you at unexpected moments delights us and inspires the younger members of our family to live up to your example. What a worthwhile legacy you leave for those who are to follow!

And so tomorrow as you descend the stage steps, as the strains of "Pomp and Circumstance" accompany your last grade-school procession, your father and I will send you our silent prayer over the heads of the onlookers. It will be a prayer of congratulations, of pride, of happiness mingled with an inevitable catch in the throat. For tomorrow your new life begins--and you are more than ready to meet it.

We will share your triumph from a distance, beloved child, as all good parents must do. And we will try--oh, so very hard--not to cry.

Mom

SUMMER

Dear Diary,

It's here again, another summer vacation. Lazy days lying out in the sun, hot dogs and lemonade, golf games and swimming.

Then there's my schedule.

Try as I may, I usually approach summer with consternation. My world spins even faster now, with interruptions in the routine; constant noise from daytime TV, stereo, and arguments; toys and clothing covering every surface, and the plaintive whine of children who have "nothing to do-o-o." What am I to do when my car disappears down the street (someone forgot to mention his job schedule) or Husband surveys the disaster scene and asks what I've been doing all day?

On the other hand, summer can also be the best of times. The weather is definitely on our side--sweet mellow breezes bending the weeping willow boughs, the soft expectant hush of sunrise, days filled with unlimited possibilities. There is time in summer, languid golden hours for conversation and sharing with the older kids, who've been too rushed to communicate all year; time to enjoy the younger gang as they enjoy the sunshine; time for an unhurried evening stroll with Spouse.

I suppose, Diary, that summer is just like life--so much depends on how you look at it. And too often I find myself focusing on the negatives, and neglecting the promising potential hiding on the other side of the coin.

We women are especially prone to this outlook, I find. We tend to focus on the flaws in our marriages, rather than rejoicing that the two of us are still together, still trying in a culture that often works against our values. We consider our children's lapses as proof of our own failures (their triumphs, however, are strictly luck). We are hardest on ourselves, beating our breasts in guilt and shame whenever we fall short of the goals those nameless "experts" have set for us.

And yet, what is our ultimate goal in this world? Is it not to minister to others--and yes, to ourselves, too--as Christ would have us do? With this in mind, somehow our point of view can begin to focus differently, and life can take on new meaning.

If I have resisted one temper outburst (even if submitting to another just an hour later), if I have said "yes" to a small request when I wanted to say "no," if I remembered (just once) to praise instead of blame . . . . If something I have said or done has lifted the burden of another, made someone comfortable, soothed a troubled spirit, eased loneliness, or made an individual feel better loved--then my day has been a success in the eyes of the Lord, the only "expert" who counts, no matter how many failures it has also included.

I think I'll work on that this summer, Diary. I think I'll concentrate on the tiny but important triumphs of each moment, shifting my perspective from guilt to congratulations. I'm sure it will help me make the most of summer--and the rest of my life, too.

Love,
Me

Dear Terry,

How nice that you and Kathy have taken on the responsibility of organizing the family picnic this year. You are two of my most efficient nieces, and I can imagine what a wonderful day you will provide. Of course I'll be glad to serve on the Chip 'n' Dip Committee and, since you did ask, I'll be happy to offer a few ideas of my own.

I think your selection of Loon Lake is a good choice, especially since it offers water skiing, mud wrestling, volleyball, and tennis. Does it also provide orthopedic lounge chairs for those of us in the older generation? I might advise choosing a picnic site several miles from the Penny Arcade, however; I'm sure you remember your cousin Brian who, last year, spent his entire summer allowance on Space Invaders. And make sure we are near facilities other than outhouses, Dears; it makes changing diapers so much easier.

I spoke with your Aunt Carol last week, and she will again be responsible for the games. We thought we might drop "Pin the Tail on the Donkey" (remember last year when your cousin Brian zapped Uncle Joe on a place which shall remain nameless?), but she will provide water-filled balloons, blindfolds, sacks for the races, and several raw eggs. All poker chips and playing cards will, however, be confiscated.

As to food, I think you're wise to suggest that every family bring their own. It just isn't fair to expect Cousin Mike, Mary Ann, and the baby to provide as much fried chicken as Aunt Patty, who's used to cooking for ten or twelve every night. Besides, we always sample each other's goodies, anyway. I do think we ought to keep the watermelon under lock and key till the last minute, though. And this year, perhaps you could persuade someone to bring salt, pepper, mustard, and something to drink.

I hear that Uncle Jim is fully recovered from last year's touch football game (apparently his neck brace was removed this month) and is eagerly awaiting a rematch with all the nephews. My own sons have promised to go easy on him; now if you can both get the same commitment from your brothers, perhaps we won't have to bother those nice paramedics again.

I'm glad Aunt Rita will send out those cleverly illustrated invitations once more, but could you possibly get someone else to draw the map? Last year our family ended up in the state of Michigan, and I'm sure that wasn't her intention. Was I, maybe, holding it upside down? And as to insect repellent, why not just make up some in gallon jugs with spray attachments? (I'll be sure to keep Brian occupied elsewhere.) It beats having to wear mosquito netting all day.

That about covers it, gals. I'm assuming you're banning all transistor radios, portable TVs, and Cousin Tom's drum set from the festivities and will provide sticks along with the marshmallows this year. If so, there's nothing else for me to do but make twenty-five pounds of potato salad and convince your Uncle Bill to join us.

See you on the big day.

Aunt Joanie

June 6

Dear Repairman:

This is to inform you that I am having a slight problem with my typewriter. In case you haven't already noticed, the ''R'' key seems to be sticking. I would appreciate your fixing this machine as soon as possible. I am a free-lance writer, and it is difficult to compose stories and articles that do not require the use of an ''R.''

Sincerely,
Mrs. Anderson

June 13

Dear Service Manager:

On June 6 I brought the enclosed typewriter in for servicing. Today it was returned to me, completely cleaned, oiled, and with the ''R'' key replaced, at a cost of $44.75. Somewhere along the way, however, the ribbon appears to have gotten mangled. And the space bar will not depress without coaxing. I would appreciate your looking into this matter at your earliest convenience. I find it difficult to run my free-lance writing business without a functioning ribbon and space bar.

Sincerely,
Mrs. Anderson

June 19

Dear Product ion   Su per vi sor :

On June 18, I rece ived the enclosed typewr iter back
from   your serv ice manager . He had replac ed both
the mangl ed ribbon and the   space bar and al so
clean ed and oiled the machine at   a   cost of
$71. 75. However, I am now noticing a strange
ski pping tendency, and the c arriage return seems a
bit shaky,
    too.
 This delemma is dri ving me cra zy. Can you
 H ELP?

Sin cerely,
Mrs . Ander son

June 25

Dear Corporation President:

This is to inform you that on June 29 I will be
picketing your northwest suburban store, along with
some neighbors and family members who are
sympathetic to my plight. The matter concerns a two-
year-old typewriter which I have sent in for servicing
on three separate occasions (to the tune of $139.50)
and which, at this point, is totally useless due to the
fact that it was returned to me with half the keyboard
missing.
I am using a borrowed machine to inform you of our
protest march. The typewriter in question will be hung
in effigy outside the store at approximately 2 PM (or
whenever the TV crews arrive). I have also contacted
the Better Business Bureau, our Chamber of Commerce,

the pastor of my church, my congressman, and my
writers' club members, several of whom will be
discussing the merits of your typewriters with
reporters from our local newspaper.
See you on the six o'clock news.

Not so sincerely,
Mrs. Anderson

June 29

Dear President:

The new typewriter arrived yesterday, in plenty of time
for me to cancel our protest march, and I'd like to
thank you for your prompt attention to this matter. It
warms my heart to know that there are business
executives Out There who really care . . . .
The typewriter has all its keys, a functioning ribbon
and space bar, and also types without skipping. I am a
bit concerned, however, with the machine's tendency
to bounce off the desk and into my lap whenever I
reach a speed of more than twenty words per minute.
What say you? Shall I type slower, or do we chance the
service center again?
Oh, and by the way, the "R" key sticks.

Sincerely,
Mrs. Anderson

June 25

Dear Dad,

As you remember, I was usually bored with history as a child, especially when it concerned our family. I knew that Mom hailed from Iowa, and you had grown up in the same Chicago neighborhood in which we were being raised, but that was as far as my interest went. There seemed nothing more tedious than listening to you and Mom trace the lineage of a distant relative and when, at family picnics, our elders began reminiscing about "the good old days," we kids immediately scattered to the ball field.

I don't know when I first became aware of the gaps in my knowledge of my background--or more importantly, when I began to care about the gaps. Perhaps it started when my own youngsters realized that they were the sixth generation to grow up in the same community and began to ask questions I couldn't answer. Maybe the success of TV's "Roots" whetted my interest, or a faraway relative writing for information on a family tree her clan was compiling. Whatever the catalyst, I began to understand that I was missing some vital links with my past. And when one of your brothers died, an uncle who'd shared marvelous memories with us kids (when we'd cared enough to listen), it became clear that stories of our ancestors would soon slip away forever if something wasn't done.

You, Dad, provided the answer. Seeing our growing interest in the past, you spent several months in quiet research and scribbling, then presented each of your offspring with a tape you had recorded. On it was the story of your life.

I cannot describe the feelings I experienced when I listened to the tape for the first time. You traced your lineage, described the history of many familiar neighborhood landmarks, and offered an intriguing collection of anecdotes about your early childhood. The tape was rich in details of the past, but for me it was far more than that. Seen through the eyes of a dear parent, discussed in your own voice, our family background became a priceless gift, a sharing of self that no history book could ever duplicate.

Subsequent playings of the tape have provided my own family with many warm moments. Your grandchildren are fascinated with Grandpa's references to prices--your family home renting for $15 per month, a truckload of cabbage once sold by a farmer for 50 cents "because we picked them ourselves." The unheated attic bedroom where you sometimes awakened with a thin layer of ice on the blankets, the tinker who came twice a year to fix what needed fixing, the story of your first train ride into the big city--such episodes paint exciting word-pictures for us. And we marvel at the changes your generation has witnessed-- from outhouses to modern appliances, from the invention of the crystal radio set to color TV, from the horse and buggy to man on the moon. Listening to your voice matter-of-factly sketching the progression of society, Dad, we are struck by the awesome adaptability your generation demonstrated.

Past events can be found recorded in any historical chronicle. What makes your tape so special is that it is the story of us, our own place in the past, the events that shaped our father and through him, his children and grandchildren. We understand now, much more fully, the unique contribution our family has made.

If I had my way, such a project would be undertaken by every family. Photographs and written history are, of course, intriguing. But there is nothing to compare with the sound of a familiar and beloved voice, telling a story in his or her own words. Whether painstakingly researched or simply narrated as each thought comes to mind, the resulting tape is a mixture of facts blended with memory, a precious gift to be shared and cherished forever.

Trust you to give <u>us</u> a Father's Day present, Dad. Thank you so very much.

Love,
Your daughter

Dear Sis,

It was great chatting with you last week. (It's a wonder the telephone company didn't cut us off--isn't there a law against three-hour long-distance calls?) You asked, typically, if we wouldn't consider spending our summer vacation at your house, and I suppose it's time to explain why my answer is always "no." It has nothing to do with you and your kind hospitality, Sis; it's just that--until we reach Social Security status-- Husband and I have decided to forego the annual summer extravaganza.

I have to admit it was easier when the children were little. I have fond memories of that week we all shared at Lake Minnetonka (even though we discovered that our idea of vacation living is to have all small-fry fed, bathed, and bedded by 7 PM, and yours is to begin barbecuing the evening meal in time for the Late Show). Sharing a rented cabin is fun, inexpensive, and (until the gang inevitably comes down with chicken pox) an easy escape from duties on the home front.

But our children are no longer little, and spending a week building sand castles at water's edge does not appeal to my six-foot-tall teens (especially if the cabin's electrical power cannot be depended upon for three hair driers, simultaneously blowing). Then, too, our choice of vacation leisure activities is a matter of great debate: Do we wish to spend our evenings at auto shows (checking out the latest design in carburetors) or rock concerts (checking out the latest design in raggy jeans)? Do our teenagers wish to spend their afternoons at Kiddieland, the Choo-Choo Museum, or (our favorite) the Junior Petting Zoo? Do we rent several cars so that everyone can take advantage of his or her own pursuits? But isn't this supposed to be a family vacation? (And in which vehicle will the child with the problem of car sickness be tolerated?)

But, you point out reasonably, if we visit your home, there'll be plenty of opportunities for everyone's activities. True, but you're forgetting that we must first get to your house. Financing a jet trip for our gang would rival the national debt. (And I have no desire to repeat the episode when, our flight canceled, we sat in an airport for eight hours listening to the three year old sing "The Teddy Bear's Picnic" every fifteen minutes, interspersed with "Is this our vacation, Mommy?") And a ten-hour car ride leaves something to be desired, too. Our six-person sedan is more than adequate for our seven-person family, provided that no one breathes too deeply or looks at another ("Mother-r-r, he's teasing me!"), needs the services of a roadside rest area ("But Dad, I hafta go now!"), or plans to eat or doze along the way ("Get your elbow out of my eye!" "Who took the last peanut-butter-and-bologna sandwich?" "Mother-r-r!"). The money saved on this close-knit venture is usually splurged on family counseling upon our return.

Then there's the challenge of packing for the clan. Carrying along an adequate supply of food is a must (cheaper than restaurant fare for teens who regard $2 hamburgers as appetizers). Shall the food cooler be placed in the car proper (underneath the eight year old's feet), allowing easy access (and tons of garbage) along the route? Or should it be positioned in the trunk, underneath cameras, beach balls, tennis rackets, and golf clubs? Should Mr. Eight Year Old be allowed to bring his collection of gerbil books (or, as he'd like, his collection of gerbils)? Should we position the kids in the trunk and stash the gerbils up front with us? Should I keep the carsick child's medication within easy reach (and the child himself at a far distance)? And Husband did remember to load the seven suitcases. Didn't he?

Okay, I can hear your calm reply, if your house is too far away, why not settle for a quicker trip--say, two or three nights at a resort? You're remembering, of course, all the years when we did just that--threw a few shirts and bathing suits into a duffel bag, pointed small-fry in the direction of the motel swimming pool, smuggled the cooler into our room, bedded the kids on the floor, and enjoyed a brief, leisurely spent break from it all. Things were simpler then, Sis. There were no video games.

Have you any idea what it's like to bring a gang of kids to a motel and tell them to "go enjoy yourselves for a few hours--Mommy and Daddy want to have a real conversation"? Do they head for the pool, the horseshoe pits, the shuffleboard court? Sorry--too tame. Instead, it's the video room where Pac-Man, Indy 500, and other electronic wonders can keep them amused indefinitely, just as long as the quarters keep coming. And there's the rub. When Husband and I totaled the bill on our last weekend, we discovered that our coin output had exceeded all other combined expenses by a whopping 50%. Which made the electronic game manufacturers ecstatic, I'm sure, but unless we can figure out a way to build a mint in the basement, our dream of a "simple, economical getaway" has forever faded.

Then there's the perennial problem of Where to Go, complicated by the fact that Spouse and I have entirely different ideas on what constitutes a vacation. My own visions include breakfast in bed (upon arising at the stroke of eleven), several good novels near a beach chair (preferably on a deserted beach), dining and dancing at a local posh spot each evening, and an occasional shopping trip to break the sweet monotony.

As Husband points out, I could accomplish all of this at home (if only they would let me).

Needless to say, my Better Half has other ideas. After a rousing predawn four-mile hike (capped by a vigorous swim), he's ready to greet a day of sight-seeing, even more exciting if a mountain or swamp is somehow involved. By 6:30 PM he is curled comfortably in front of the TV, eyes already drooping, asking why I would possibly want to go out now when he's feeling so relaxed and cozy. (Complicate this scene by inserting images of several offspring--playing transistor radios, locking each other in the bathroom, and asking whether we can eat at McDonald's or Burger King tonight.)

No, Sis, we've made up our minds. Husband will play golf with our teens several times this summer, we'll take the family out for a luncheon or two, spend a day at a local amusement park, and host several neighborhood barbecues. But climb into the car for a togetherness journey into the great unknown?

Not until the grandchildren come along. If they misbehave, we can always send them home.

Thanks anyway,
Me

Dear Time Management Consultant,

It was a pleasure for me to be in the audience at your recent library lecture. (I was the woman in the red knee socks who arrived about twenty minutes late and had to climb over that bearded gentleman in the third row.) I've always wanted to learn how to make every minute count, and I'm glad your speech was directed at the normal average housewife. However, I do have a few questions and hope you will have the time (Ha! ha!) to indulge me.

1. You suggest "always doing two things at once," such as doing mending while on the telephone or playing French language cassettes while driving. Unfortunately, I have not been able to locate my sewing box since 1978, and if you were ever a passenger in my car, I'm sure you'd be shouting, "For Pete's sake, keep your attention on the road!" just like everyone else does.

I am wondering if ironing a Girl Scout uniform while baking an angel food cake while timing a load in the drier while supervising the toddler's bath while listening to a radio talk show while arguing with the ten year old qualifies as doing "two things at once." If so, I'm farther ahead than I thought.

2. Honestly, your idea about setting up a central work station in the kitchen was excellent. Imagine-- some women really do keep checkbook, message pads (different color paper for each family member), envelopes, stamps, grocery coupons, address book, and pens all in the same spot! I'm hard pressed to duplicate this feat; our messages usually get written on newspaper margins with chalk (and then get lost if

we've run out of those banana and lettuce refrigerator magnets). Stamps and pens are kept in a locked safe, free from the fingers of small looters (unfortunately, the safe is at the bank), and the checkbook is (I think) at the bottom of a purse I've been meaning to clean out (as soon as I get the time). But the work center is certainly a worthwhile goal, and I hope to establish one around the time I apply for Medicare (at least I'll have a place to file all those government forms).

3. I agree that a good manager does delegate chores. My older children wash their own clothes, keep the grass cut, run a variety of errands, and occasionally cook dinner. My problem is not in getting them to work; it is in dealing with the times they choose for said labor. When the high-schooler decides to pick up the milk on his way home from basketball practice (even though I need it now), when Mr. Ten makes hamburgers at 3 PM because he wants to "get it out of the way so I can watch the 'Mary Tyler Moore' rerun," when the lawn mower chugs at dawn and the washing machine at midnight, what is a manager to do? (Should I perhaps hire a time consultant?)

4. I have been laying out my wardrobe and accessories each evening to check for spots and loose buttons before the morning rush. However, considering my daily uniform of jeans and a T-shirt, it doesn't seem worthwhile. Should I wait until I get a real job? Or perhaps just do the housework in wool blazer and panty hose?

Thank you for your inspiring lecture, and I'll be looking forward to your reply.

The Lady in the Red Knee Socks

Dear **Coupon Club** Magazine,

You ask for readers' experiences with coupons--why they started clipping, what benefits the habit hath wrought, etc. Well, until recently I used to line the bird cage with the newspaper food section, still unread. My metal recipe box, donated by an optimistic pal at my bridal shower, remained empty except for concoctions requiring only three ingredients or less. When a bank once offered me either a floor mop or a wok as a premium, there was no contest--I gladly grabbed the mop. And when our church women's club contacted me about a cookbook fund-raiser, the caller came right to the point: "Don't worry--we wouldn't dream of asking you for a recipe; we'd just like you to write the book's foreword."

In short, my neighborhood reputation as an "un-cook" has been well established. And why not? Pots and pans aren't every woman's idea of total fulfillment. And as long as the family is well nourished, does it really matter if I nurse a secret dream of someday permanently boarding up the kitchen?

But things have changed. Maybe I got tired of thawing pork chops with a steam iron at 5:30 (and serving them with sauerkraut) because I hadn't planned ahead. Perhaps it started the day I bought ketchup because I always buy ketchup, then came home to find twelve bottles staring at me from the top shelf. Or maybe it happened when my husband glanced at the weekly supermarket tally and burst into tears. "We're spending more on groceries now than I earned fifteen years ago," he sobbed, "and there's still never anything to eat around here!" Clearly, some old habits had to fade. I was dying of terminal kitchen yawn. My family was close to revolt. Same old menus, same old dried-up bologna and generic soup. . . . Even changing a light bulb was a bigger thrill. And then we visited my sister's home for dinner.

"Should I toss out these garbage bags under the sink?" I called to her as I did the dishes. "They look jammed."

"Don't touch those!" She flew around the corner, a naked baby under her arm. "That isn't garbage--those are qualifiers."

"Qualifiers?"

"Labels and box tops and net weight statements and proof-of-purchase seals."

I stared at her. Somehow she'd always seemed so levelheaded, and too young for a mid-life crisis. "You're saving garbage?"

"It's called refunding," she corrected. "You send in whatever a company asks for, and they send you a dollar or two. Then, of course, you also use coupons when you shop. It adds up."

Light dawned. "You mean like that lady I heard about who bought $131 worth of groceries for $7.95? I thought that was a game show commercial."

"No, it's true," she assured me. "Most people don't save that much, but even ten or fifteen percent helps."

"I'd settle for a free bottle of aspirin," I sighed.

"Let's see," she rummaged through one of the bags. "I think there's an offer for free aspirin here. . . ."

From that moment on, I was hooked.

It started slowly, of course--just a subscription to a refunders' publication to find out what offers were available, a bag under the sink to hold wrappers and, of course, collecting coupons. But, like everything else in life, it soon got complicated.

"Let's see," I muttered one day at the cheese

counter, "Brand X is $1.59 and I have a 10-cent coupon, Brand Y is $1.65 with 15 cents off . . . ."

"Why not get the cheaper?" advised a little old lady, gliding past and eyeing my fistful of cutouts.

"Can't," I murmured. "Brand Z is $1.69 but there's a refund offer on it--three wrappers for a dollar. Which makes the actual price . . . let's see . . . ."

She sighed. "Or why not just forget cheese this week?"

And then there was the home front situation. "Mom, which of these is the fruit cocktail?" asked the eighth grader, holding up two identical metal cans. "Don't they make labels, anymore?"

"I sent them in on an offer," I explained, carefully shaking the cans and listening. "Here, this one is definitely fruit cocktail."

It was peas.

And the dawn I crept across the street with scissors in hand, to cut off my neighbor's rock salt label ("Send three proof-of-purchase seals--receive a Susan B. Anthony dollar!") before the garbage truck arrived. And the evening I made a spectacle out of myself at the bridge club--"You're not throwing out those gumdrop bags!" ("Mail two gumdrop bags, receive a coupon for one free bag".) Or the time I volunteered to chaperone the junior-high Christmas party just to get my hands on all those napkin labels ("Return five for $1 refund"). My spouse called it "coupon madness" and the kids referred to it as "Mom's latest hang-up." But it also produced unexpected results.

In order to find coupons, I had to study the newspaper food guide, and lo! interesting meals began appearing on the table. In order to shop efficiently for offers, I had to open cabinets, take inventory, and make a list (I didn't buy ketchup for three months). Best of all, the humdrum menus disappeared--why not try a new product if two labels brought a little check in the mail?

"You've changed," my husband mourned one day. "You're not the girl I married."

"I should hope not," I answered, efficiently cutting my way through the paper's coupon section.

"We never run out of toothpaste anymore, dinners have become interesting, we're saving money, and there's no mold growing in the refrigerator." He sighed. "There's nothing left for me to complain about."

"Old habits die hard," I soothed him. "But cheer up. I'm spending so much time in the kitchen that the ironing hasn't been done for months."

"Thanks. I needed that." He whistled his way out the door, and I returned to my shopping list. Only one more bottle of steak sauce and I'd have enough labels for a free Frisbee. . . .

As you can tell, dear editor, I'm in couponing to stay!

Sincerely,
Mrs. A.

Dear God,

I'm so worried about money.

You know it's not Florida vacations or sports cars that interest me--we've done without these items all along and have never really missed them. No, I'm scared because it's harder lately to meet the utility bills, and groceries seem to vanish in record time, and one of the kids needs orthodontia. . . . The basics of decent living seem to move farther away from us with each paycheck, Father. And I'm so worried.

Yes, I know, there are millions of your children in dire want, suffering deprivation that I cannot imagine. You've given us a world rich in food and resources, yet you must watch sadly as governments squabble and misuse your bounty. I know, too, that advertising has created "wants" that slowly become "needs" in this, the richest country in the world. Did my grandparents conceive of color TV, autos, and meat on every dinner menu as inherent constitutional rights? We have tightened our belts, Father, and given to the poor, and tried to practice conservation and common sense. But still, I'm worried.

You know that I don't care about money for my own sake. You made me a peanut butter person, content with a worn-out stuffed chair, a stack of library books, soft music, good friends. But I'm a parent, Father, and I want so much for my children. They've worked hard, supplied many of their own needs--and yet I must sometimes say, "No, we can't afford tennis lessons" or "Wear your winter coat for another year." It doesn't seem to hurt them, Father; perhaps they have become such fine people because they weren't surrounded by luxuries. But it hurts me.

And then there's my husband, approaching the time of life when pressures should slacken, responsibilities ease. Instead, he finds himself trotting more quickly on the treadmill, knowing that despite his best efforts, the checkbook will not always balance. What does this do to his pride, I wonder? How does he feel, seeing his salary spent on booster shots, tuition, new tires for the old car? He says we are worth it all and more, and I believe him. But my heart aches, and I worry.

Actually, Father, the bank balance is not my real problem; it's my pride, isn't it? I want to meet our needs in my way, through an ample income, while you, who see the whole picture, prefer to meet them in yours. I want to ''call the shots,'' to be in control, to plan and have those plans materialize. But you are asking not for my efficiency but my trust, my belief that because you made me and love me, whatever you send me is best.

Help me, Father. I will never be worry free, but you can teach me to carry my burdens with a light heart and to deal with them in the proper way. You can teach me patience, growth through trial, acceptance of your eternal plan for me.

You can teach it all, Father. Now please help me to cast aside the overdue bills and listen.

Your loving daughter

July 24

Dear Laurie,

I've stopped by your house twice this week, but as you were probably having a mad fling at the grocery store, I'm sending a note via the kids instead. Just to put your mind at rest and assure you of a peaceful vacation, YES, we would be glad to board Ping and Pong for you while you are away. Truly, I have nothing against hamsters, provided thay stay in those cheerful wire cages.

Ping and Pong will probably enjoy their visit since they'll have many members of the animal kingdom with which to play. (No, I'm not referring to the kids.) Coincidentally, we are already taking care of Winky, my sister's parrot, and although he doesn't seem too sociable (my poor husband has already had stitches on his forefinger), I imagine Winky will loosen up if I put his cage next to your hamsters'. On second thought, perhaps not--Winky does know how to unlock his door, and I wouldn't want him to investigate the hamsters too closely. Then too, Ping and Pong will have to spend much of their time on a high shelf since our beagle, Nip, is apt to be somewhat jealous. She still hasn't gotten over the shock of discovering that our sophomore is raising garter snakes in his room for a summer science project and just doesn't have time for poor old Nip right now. Honestly, sometimes dogs can have more emotional upsets than people!

I did tell you that the guppies are expecting, didn't I? We calculate that the blessed event(s) should be sometime next week, and I'm hoping that it will be a real education for the kids. Our only problem is keeping Fern, our cat, away from the tanks. I'd put her in the garage for the duration, but the baby rabbits probably wouldn't appreciate that. Of course, our fifth grader has been nagging to bring them up to his room anyway, but just between you and me, the thought of all those furry little bodies hopping around leaves me cold. I'm sure they'd irritate Winky, bother the snakes, add to poor Nip's inferiority complex, and at the very least, steal Ping's and Pong's lettuce. And, of course, we have to consider the guinea pig, too.

As usual, I've gotten off the track. Just send your hamsters over whenever convenient. We're looking forward to meeting them, and our four year old has solemnly promised to keep Hands Off!

Joan

July 25

Dear Laurie,

I quite understand that you have made other arrangements for Ping and Pong and am only sorry that we won't have the pleasure of their company. Perhaps it is for the best, however. Between searching for lost snakes and dodging bunnies, I might not have been able to give them the attention they certainly deserve.

Have a lovely vacation.

Joan

Dear Editor:

Since most of this space each day is taken up with complaints from readers--everything from the state of the union to the state of the nonfunctioning traffic signal at Third and Willow--I'd like to change the pace a bit and compliment our community.

I'm especially happy about the family activities provided by our park district, our adult education division, and various civic organizations. Such offerings keep our children busy from morning to supper time (unfortunately, no two activities are scheduled at the same time, so there is always someone hanging around the kitchen, but I admit that's my problem, not the district's).

I'm pleased with the quality of the tennis lessons this year (now if the park would only supply balls--my daughter's shots generally land in a neighboring chimney) and one of my sons is spending so much time at the pool that his locker number has been permanently retired (he's the kid who brings shampoo along to the shower room--why waste our own hot water?). Our teens enjoyed the recent Gross Sneakers contest, and I thought that giving each contestant a can of foot spray was a nice gesture (I'm amazed that our second son didn't win, however; his shoes seem held together with cellophane tape and lint).

Then there's the annual Arts and Crafts exhibit, an intriguing and interesting affair. I'm always amazed that folks can be so creative, making charming centerpieces out of dead leaves and bits of leftover macaroni, sculpting with nothing more than a few wire hangers and cola cans. We have all that stuff lying around our house, too, but it's classified as plain old debris (although the teenager's under-bed collection might be viewed as a new art form). Being noncreative, I didn't enter anything this year except the Pot Holder Competition, but I did bring home a pair of ceramic planters from the garage sale to match the two we had stored in the basement (actually, they were the same two; my husband had donated them while I was busy making my pot holders).

Even though our preschool soccer team's record was 0-9 this season, I feel it was a grand experience for my child. I'd like to publicly commend the coach for putting up with thirteen mothers, all shrieking, jumping up and down, and bursting into tears from the sidelines.

Apologies are, of course, in order to the public library (I realize our fourteen overdue books are fouling up your computer, and they will be returned just as soon as we locate them), and to the senior citizen free lunch program (my children did not read the small print on your advertising sign, and I can assure you that I do feed them, and that they will not be joining the senior citizens again). I'd also like to congratulate our school administrator for devising such an interesting junior-high science summer session--I had no idea that such a small amount of gunpowder could make such a large bang.

Anyway, dear Editor, I appreciate the chance to offer a public thanks. Isn't it better to see something positive in this space, for a change?

Sincerely,
A Pleased Citizen

P.S. Anyone wanting to join our newly formed Pothole Protest Committee or interested in picketing the train station this weekend, please contact me.

Dear Ginny,

Yes, you're right, and so is the neighborhood gossip--there was some excitement at our house this week. Believe it or not, we were asked to be one of the rating families, those invisible souls who decide what's worth watching on TV and what isn't.

Arbitron Ratings Service may never include us again. But after all, it was their idea--not ours. And how else can the nation learn which shows are hits and which are duds without the cooperation of outstanding families like ours? Along with humming "America, the Beautiful" at least once a week and campaigning for cleaner sewers, I regard keeping a TV ratings diary as my patriotic duty.

Actually, if I had been home the morning that the ratings lady phoned, my first impulse would have been to veto her suggestion. I have enough to do around here, what with reading magazines and talking on the phone all day, without also keeping track of the boob tube and its mesmerized audience.

However, it was my civic-minded husband who answered the call and accepted the challenge (knowing full well that he would be away from the house during most of the week in question).

In his helpful way, Husband also informed Ms. Arbitron that we owned five TV sets, so naturally she forwarded five viewing diaries. Unfortunately, two of those sets have been collecting mold in our garage since 1972, awaiting the day when a junk dealer will recognize their true potential, and a third set works well if one does not consider a picture tube essential to pleasant viewing.

So there I was, already perpetrating a fraud on the unsuspecting public, with five diaries and only two-and-a-half working sets. But the most significant revelations were yet to come. For we discovered, as we began our viewing log, that our TV tastes, along with our political views, lawn sprinkling habits, and pizza preferences were light years removed from the American mainstream.

Our choices for Saturday morning, for example--"Sylvester and Tweety" followed by "Tarzan, Lord of the Jungle"--seemed singularly lacking in imagination and not destined to spark any trends. Discovering that our teenagers preferred "Dick Van Dyke" reruns to the five o'clock news was an academic humiliation we would have given anything to avoid reporting.

Would advertisers be impressed with the fact that as the "unemployed" woman of the household, I preferred working on my waxy yellow buildup to even one game show? What about prime time, when the Top Ten bit the dust in favor of educational offerings such as "Animal Kingdom" or "Fun with Social Security"?

How would Arbitron interpret the upstairs TV diary which, on two successive evenings, showed identical entries as the downstairs TV diary? Would they condemn us for both a waste of energy and a failure to communicate? There was no place on the form to explain that if I've told the twelve year old once, I've told him a MILLION TIMES to take out the garbage, and that since he forgot again, he can darn well rot in that bedroom. . . .

There was also no opportunity to mention that those erasure smudges on the downstairs diary involved my discovery that the third grader was logging not only his own viewing hours, but also those of the four gerbils.

Worse, diary-keepers were expected to report not only the program choices of the family but also of any guest who might wander in. "Now, let's see," I mused one afternoon, "Paul and Jimmy watched part of 'The Brady Bunch' . . . ."

"So did I," Sixth grader mentioned helpfully.

"I know, but you're already listed in the diary. I have to write in Paul and Jimmy."

"Paul didn't watch 'The Brady Bunch.'"

"He didn't?"

"Uh, uh. He was upstairs watching 'Leave It to Beaver.'"

"No, he wasn't," the third grader pointed out. "He had a fight with Jimmy and left. David was watching 'Leave It to Beaver.'"

"David?" I asked. "Was he here today? I didn't even notice him."

"You were on the phone, calling Stephanie's mother."

"That's right. I was trying to find out if Stephanie glanced at 'Family Feud' or 'Sesame Street' when she dropped off that brownie recipe."

"My gerbils like 'Family Feud.'"

Even more challenging were my neighborhood search missions to track down the offspring who came in, turned on the TV, made himself a peanut-butter-and-pickle sandwich, and then exited, leaving the set blaring with only the drapes as an audience.

"Just how long did you watch 'Captain Kangaroo'?" I finally caught up with Third Son on the corner pitcher's mound.

"Gosh, Mom, not now! We're in the middle of the series playoffs . . . ."

"Play ball!" the umpire shouted. "And get that woman off the field."

"One segment or two?" I insisted, pencil poised.

"Hey guys, get this!" screamed the second baseman. "Our pitcher watches 'Captain Kangaroo'!"

"I'm ruined," moaned Third Son.

"One segment or two?"

Actually, Arbitron did us a favor by forcing us to examine our viewing habits. We discovered that Miss Under-Four and Mr. Over-Forty were both watching too often, and they have now embarked on an after-dinner jogging program together. We found that our high school sophomore can simultaneously wear a transistor plug, talk on the phone, read a magazine, and still log an hour of Howard Cosell. And we also discovered that in order to record every fifteen-minute segment on two-and-a-half TVs for seven people during a one-week period, one must either hire a genie or grow six more arms.

All in all, Ginny, we're grateful to have become a part of the American survey system. But should Arbitron consider asking us again, I hope they think it over very carefully. As you know, the gerbils had babies last week.

Bye for now,
Joan

August 10

Dear Ms. Katherine,

Just a note to thank you for your estimate on redoing the living and dining rooms. I'm sorry that we got our signals mixed--I thought I'd made it clear that we were planning to do all our own painting, and the carpet and drapes were definitely staying. What we needed were suggestions on how to pull the rooms together, add eye appeal, make a statement--oh, you know how it's put in the House Beautiful magazines.

However, since the only statement you felt capable of making was, "Throw everything out and start over!" we will seek help elsewhere. . . .

August 13

Dear Mr. Charles,

Thank you for your visit to our living and dining rooms and for your helpful ideas. Unfortunately, we will have to keep our couch and dining room set, but I will take your suggestion of a corner wing chair under advisement (which is where it will probably stay; my husband is not fond of wing chairs, especially those that cost $500--my car was less than that).

What we are attempting to do is liven up the area with some small touches, but we don't know where to start. Since the challenge is apparently too much for you, too, we will continue our search. . . .

August 16

Dear Madam Madge,

I appreciate your suggestion of a new grand piano to add interest to the far wall in our living room; however, the old upright has served us well and will have to stay (actually, how does one get a grand piano through the average front door?). I do realize that the room needs a focal point, but I was thinking of something a bit more modest, say, a new plastic plant.

Since our minds obviously aren't in tune, we'll ask someone else. . . .

August 19

Dear Sue,

Why didn't I start with you? Anyone who has a house as cute as yours ought to know something about decorating (and soothing disgruntled husbands).

Imagine--four $1.98 plumes stuck in a big glass bottle, several hanging baskets, new frames for all those old family snapshots--and the job's done!

Now, can you help me with the hallway? Please?

Love,
Joan

Dear Patsy,

Your letter was a joy, but was it really necessary to enclose photos of the family cavorting on the Colorado slopes? Yes, I know you can't help the fact that the midwest is stuck in the middle of a record-breaking heat wave, but I really didn't need the reminder of crisp, clean snow and icy-cold sparkling streams, old pal. Especially now. (Didn't I write this same letter last March?)

You ask how our summer has been, and just for that (and because I desperately need someone over three feet tall to talk to), I'll tell you:

--It's been sand, sand everywhere. In our beds, on the bottom of the bathtub, inside my sneakers, embedded in the rugs. And crumbs, taking possession of the kitchen counters, marching across the dishwasher, lying on the floor to be crunched underfoot. I have posted signs, explaining the purpose of a sponge, and even conducted a class called "Cleaning a Kitchen Can Be Fun," but they continue to outwit me (both crumbs and offspring). Dare I hope for a morning when twenty-five dirty glasses do not stare at me from the depths of a greasy sink? Most of them encrusted with either crumbs or sand?

--It's been kids, ringing our doorbell by the dawn's early light, cluttering up the front walk with bikes and wagons, coming in to use the bathroom (wet swimming suits dripping on crumb-covered floors), or phoning their mothers to ask if they might stay for supper (nobody asked me). It's been gangs on the second floor listening to rock music, crowds on the porch playing Old Maid, groups in the driveway fighting over hopscotch rules. It's been Mother, remembering the days B.C. (Before Children) when I vowed that the kids' friends would always be welcome at our home. And wondering if vows can be broken without consulting a lawyer.

--It's been lemonade, a gallon pitcher mixed each morning and replenished before supper. And Daddy buying stock in a lemon farm and complaining because there's never any left for him.

--It's been sports equipment--golf bags lying in the hallway so Mother can sprain her other ankle (did I tell you I've started jogging?). Tennis balls being "freshened" in the drier, and rackets placed carefully on the couch so Daddy will sit on them and turn the air blue with language not heard since last winter's Superbowl game. It's been soccer shoes left in the driveway to be run over by Daddy's car (more blue air) and baseball mitts and bats left on some ball field ("I'll remember where I lost them, Mom--honest!"). And Mother remembering the days B.C. when healthy competition seemed like such a good idea.

--It's been telephones, starting their urgent summons during corn flakes and juice, and still calling us as the Late Show ends. Messages taped to the refrigerator ("Dad, some man called--please call him back") and shouts to the second floor ("Timmy--you're supposed to be at work--now!"). And trying to be patient as the seventh or eighth little voice inquires as to Small Daughter's whereabouts. And finally, refusing to answer the phone at all, only to later discover that Husband was trying to ask me out to dinner.

--It's been smells, the mouth-watering aroma of barbecued meat, the rich flavor of damp dirt in the vegetable garden mingling with pungent pepper leaves and crisp tomatoes, the soft, satisfying scent of a summer rose--and the ever-present whiff of detergent accompanying the endless chug-splash of our faithful clothes washer.

--And finally, it's been shopping trips--pencil boxes, paper, neat new school clothes signaling the beginning of orderly days and the end of freedom.

--It's been quiet, restless, exhausting, interesting, endless, yet all too fleeting. Soon summer green will give way to autumn brown, and peace and routine will reign once more. I will welcome the return of these comforting, familiar hours, the chance for orderly activity and discovery and growth. . . .

But a part of me will remain beneath the willow tree, soothed in memory by the magic music of summer. . . .

Enjoy your frostbite, Patsy. Good hearing from you.

Best,
Your pal

August 30

Dear Mrs. Walsh,

Today I gave my daughter into your care, this mighty mite of exuberance who has brightened our family's life in such a glowing way. I was proud and yet a little tearful, too, when she went to you, took your hand, and never looked back as you led her to the toy corner. Standing rather uncertainly by the kindergarten door, I watched other mothers and children engaged in this first farewell and wondered if she would turn around just one last time, blow me a kiss before I stepped out into my new and alien life.

How did she grow up so fast, Mrs. Walsh? How did she gain so much poise and confidence in these incredibly short five years? Didn't I hold her closely just yesterday, cuddly pink blanket wrapping a tiny miracle of love? Didn't I guide her first tottering steps, play patty-cake and peekaboo, show her the wonder of butterflies and beetles on a sultry, seemingly-infinite summer afternoon?

But it was not infinite, was it? Slowly, stealthily, the hours passed, claiming another day, yet another small portion of her babyhood. Tiny white shoes giving way to battered sneakers, rubber duckies being abandoned for doll houses and bikes, moving from "dada" and "mama" to a commentary on the relative merits of green VS red popsicles. And I was not ready for the change.

There were times, of course, when I looked forward to this day with all my heart, wanting for her the pleasures she would discover in the classroom, dreaming of the thick and lovely silence surrounding me at last. But the dreaming has become bittersweet, for I have gained my solitude at a price too high to pay.

But pay it I must, of course, for this is a mother's role. Love must be fluid, always moving, ever changing as a child slips slowly into the waiting world. This morning I was cheerful as we chose her colorful new clothes, laughing as she carefully assembled paper, crayons, and "show-and-tell" toy, calm as she slipped her trusting hand in mine for the long walk to the schoolroom door. "Don't go," I wanted to whisper on the way. "Stay a child forever! There is too much waiting for you out there, and I cannot protect you from it all!"

But I did not speak, of course. Mothers know how to examine a fallen leaf or high-flying plane, to hide the tears in their eyes. We have done it for so many years, at so many different doors. And perhaps the children never know. . . .

So now she is yours, Mrs. Walsh, this bouncy, sometimes bossy, always curious child of God. Cherish her, care for her, love her as well as you can. For you are her first link with the waiting world, her first experience with the life that we will share, more and more, only from a distance.

Make it a good beginning, Mrs. Walsh. Handle these precious and vulnerable children with patience and love during this most important year. My prayers are with you, and with kindergarten teachers everywhere. How much--how very much--we need you.

That little girl's mother

AUTUMN

Dear Diary,

Okay, it's definitely time to get organized. Even though the calendar heralds a new beginning each January, we mothers know that the real year starts in autumn. We banish the summer season to drawers and storage cabinets, packing away bathing suits and fertilizer with enthusiasm, and clothe ourselves in brisk efficiency once again. We are ready, but for what?

Autumn is the time of goal setting, reevaluation, the chance to take stock, see where we are--and where we might like to be. It holds the promise of new beginnings, but it can also be a very difficult time, especially for women. Prodded as we are by media and social change, many of us feel pressured to accomplish, to do, and yet at what cost to the life we have already carefully built and nurtured?

Perhaps I will again choose the compromise solution, the one which has become so meaningful and satisfying over the years. Again this month I will make out my annual list, putting down all the things I wish to learn or do, all the dreams I have deferred until more peaceful days are reached. It is hard, this list, because I must analyze myself as a separate entity, not linked to those who make up my world. I must consider my own needs, desires, goals--and list them without regard to others. We tend to think of this process as selfish, and yet we must remember that unless we put something into ourselves, we will eventually have nothing to take out and offer to others.

Once I have composed my "Want List," I will think about it while my hands are busy with routine chores.

I will consider each entry and what that choice will mean to me and to those around me. And then I will make a selection, put this new challenge into my life-- and see where it leads.

How well I remember the autumn when I chose "Writing" as my new goal. Could I have imagined that the hour a day spent on this pursuit would eventually lead me to such a rich and satisfying career? Or the season that I selected a Scripture study course--the challenge of being back in a classroom setting, unraveling the mysteries of the Old Testament, deepening my understanding and love of my Christian heritage.

There were choices that did not work out and had to be abandoned because of disinterest or failure. But these experiences, too, were worthwhile, for they taught me more about myself. And such knowledge is always valuable, whatever the outcome.

Every woman needs to carve out a private piece of world for herself, one in which she can experiment, learn, fail, or triumph. It is the way we continue to grow, to reach toward God and others, to make the most of what we have been given. Perhaps this year I'll join a volunteer group working to keep a food bank supplied. Or take my turn on a local help hot line. Maybe I'll decide to read every Agatha Christie novel in the library, or finally--FINALLY--learn to swim.

The choice itself (and its outcome) is not as important as the decision to choose. Before me lies opportunity, excitement, challenge, the chance to say "yes" to a brand new experience. Just a few hours each week, invested in me, can pay a wealth of dividends.

So long for now, Diary. It's time to make my list.

Love,
Me

Dear Instructor,

As a member in good standing of Beginner Body
Rhythms Class (at least I have not, as yet, been carried
out of the gym by the paramedics), I would like to take
this opportunity to share a few of my thoughts with
you. You do occasionally ask for comments from the
floor (which is where we usually are--gasping and
moaning softly), and it is only my extreme fear of
fainting in front of the others that has kept me from
speaking out thus far. (I do hate to make a nuisance
out of myself.)

Last week you asked several women why they signed
up for Body Rhythms. I've pondered that question
myself, particularly when I bend to retrieve something
from under the kitchen sink and my bones sound as
though I am popping corn. The answer, actually, is
simple: When a woman who has taken her thinness for
granted all her life suddenly looks down and discovers
that she has unconsciously been carrying her
midsection around in her arms, something must be
done. I had no intention of waiting until my thighs
developed rope burn. It was now or never, and your
class seemed an answer to a prayer.

However, I'm having some adjustment problems. I've
never been the athletic type--riding a ten-speed bike,
which allows my thumb a peppy workout changing
gears, has always seemed to me to be adequate
exercise. Further, after the park district crew got
together and banned me from the tennis courts (they
were tired of retrieving balls from trees, and the
spectators were dying of boredom), I gave up
completely. You will, therefore, understand why I find

some of the class exercises absolutely impossible to perform. It's one thing to jog around the gym to a rock record while chanting the class motto: "A minute in my mouth! An hour in my stomach! A lifetime on my hips!" But the routine where one must touch her forehead to her toes while giving her neighbor a back rub--well, really! My feet happen to be made of clay, not rubber.

Actually, the whole experience can seem downright intimidating to an onlooker. On the first morning of class, a gang of us were lined up in the hall when suddenly a strange woman clutched my arm. "Look," she croaked in horror, staring into the gym where a group of women were, somehow, balancing on one shoulder while the rest of their bodies arched precariously into thin air. The expressions of stoic suffering on their faces was something to behold. "Oh, my," murmured the strange woman. "We aren't going to do that, are we?"

"I think it's an optical illusion," I tried to reassure her. "And besides, that's the advanced class."

But it was no use. As I watched, she backed quietly down the corridor, turned, and fled out the door. I'll say this for her--that woman could really run.

Therefore, I think you should consider closing the gym door until advanced classes are over. As I understand the principle of this thing, participants aren't supposed to have heart attacks until after they've exercised.

I suppose by now you've noticed that I am the only one in the class still wearing a "Woman Power" T-shirt, yellow pedal pushers, and white socks instead of the regulation skintight leotard. I'm not trying to be antisocial; it's just that I believe certain things should be left to the imagination, things like hips, stomachs, thighs. . . . I'm perfectly willing to expose my elbows to public scrutiny (they haven't yet begun to sag or wither), but as for the rest--well, give me a good old full-length Indian sari any day, complete with veil, if possible.

I have to applaud your goals for us, of course, and the enthusiastic manner in which you lead us in those deep knee bends, breathing exercises, and the Twist. I can't imagine where anyone gets the energy to scream, "Go to it, gals!" while walking on her fingertips, but it's an inspiring sight. And your oft-repeated slogan, "A size eight dress by Christmas! Even if you have to wear one on each leg!" brings tears to my eyes.

And so I'll keep signing in, even though I seem to be developing a sort of palsy in my right hand. Fighting the battle of the bulge is a never-ending struggle (especially when I'm having trouble rolling out of bed in the morning). And I promise to continue my chin-ups, rope jumping, and arabesques at home, whenever the family isn't looking (and whenever the agony from my newly-acquired slipped disc isn't too acute).

Yes, exercising is certainly wonderful. Especially when I can stop.

Sincerely,
Ms. Woman Power

September 20-24

MONDAY CHORE CHART

Tim--Vacuum family room, scrape gum off end
   table (yes, it's your gum).
Chris--Bring down boxes blocking stairwell.
   Dispose of same.
Billy--Carry up clean laundry, put on everyone's
   beds.
Brian--Make beds.

TUESDAY CHORE CHART

Billy--Sort clean laundry on everyone's floors.
   Figure out where it all belongs. Put it there!
Brian--Carry out garbage. Stay out.
Tim--Pick up Monopoly game, Tinker toys, and
   chess sets in living room. Look for pieces
   under piano.
Chris--Move boxes blocking back door. Dispose
   of same.

   Anyone want to polish furniture?

WEDNESDAY CHORE CHART

Tim--Go to store for bread and aspirin.

Billy--Clean upstairs bathroom. Also clean tub,
washstand, toilet, mirror, and floor. Also
remove dirty towels and underwear. Also find
a new bar of soap.

Chris--Get boxes out of my closet this minute
and dispose of same before I dispose of you.

Brian--Empty all wastebaskets. Into garbage.

Nancy--Pick up toys.

Anyone want to polish furniture?

THURSDAY CHORE CHART

Chris--Remove golf clubs, bowling shoes, and
basketball from downstairs bathroom. Put in
garage.

Tim--Polish furniture.

Brian--Go to store for aspirin.

Billy--Carry up clean laundry. Place on beds. Do
not make beds.

Nancy--Pick up toys.

FRIDAY CHORE CHART

Everyone stay outside until pizza gets here.

September 29

Dear Emily (Post) and Julia (Child),

The first party I ever threw as a newlywed was so dull that even my husband left early. On the second occasion our merrymaking awakened our baby, who proceeded to throw up all over the guests' coats, tossed across our bed. During the third attempt, my husband decided at the last minute to barbecue the meat outside, and I finally served dinner at 1:45 AM. With a record like that, only a fool would keep on trying.

But I do. Somewhere there has to be a magic formula that makes entertaining as simple as falling off an hors d'oeuvre. And a lot more fun. However, I haven't found it yet. (Send ideas quickly--we're entertaining tonight!)

Other women don't seem to have my problem. One neighbor can feed her husband's bowling team on a moment's notice simply by thawing the marvelous homemade goodies always stocked in her freezer. Another sets her table with gleaming crystal, untarnished silver, and real roses bobbing around in a bowl of pink water. Last week I tossed a plastic daisy into a pickle jar, but somehow it didn't have the same appeal.

Part of my dilemma stems from a confused sense of priorities. Should a hostess concentrate mainly on her house, making sure that guests do not spy water pistols in the bathtub, or dirty socks sticking out from under the buffet? (That's the direction I took this past week, and none of the children are speaking to me at present.) Or is a beautifully served dinner the most important component of a gracious evening? Once I managed to accomplish both of these feats at the same time, but since I had forgotten to mail the invitations, the event lost something of its luster.

One must also tread gently when making up a guest list. I once invited three couples from our new neighborhood over for cocktails and discovered as the doorbell rang that two of them hadn't spoken to each other in ten years. It was a very brief cocktail hour. On another occasion my mother brought her elderly maiden aunt over on the same day that we had asked a family with eight children to picnic with us. Fortunately, my great-aunt has a sense of humor (and a hearing aid, which she kept on "OFF" throughout the day) or it could have been dismal.

Another problem is arranging appropriate decorations. It helps if a hostess is naturally creative and has good finger coordination, but I have only recently learned to press the "ON" button on our washing machine and would not classify myself as particularly inventive. Buying a batch of Happy Birthday napkins is about as festive as I can get. Especially if they are misplaced until Valentine's Day.

Since we have become homeowners, our family usually hosts the holiday get-togethers so popular with our clan, and these, too, have had their disastrous moments. One of the problems is that stray relatives seem to pop up at the last minute, necessitating a quick shuffle with place settings and extra water added to the soup. A miscalculation can result in everyone's favorite uncle consuming Thanksgiving turkey in the laundry room because no one remembered to dash off a place card for him.

Actually, a too short table can turn out to be a blessing since our extended family is prone to political arguments. Last Christmas, cleverly sensing the impending battle, my mother, sister, and I enjoyed our dinner on TV trays in the den, far from the shouting over socialism and property taxes. A bit unorthodox, but definitely peaceful.

Another reason why I approach family dinners with the enthusiasm of a tortoise is because my female relatives are all so creative in the kitchen. I'm the only one who finds it impossible to recite the recipe for curried rutabaga from memory, or whip up a scratch wedding cake while chatting on the phone. My relatives smile kindly over my barbecued-beef-and-orange-Jell-O menus, but I suspect their hearts are really not in it.

Friends, on the other hand, have all accepted this deficiency in my character and are always willing to help in a crisis (or suggest pot luck, if they are to be invited). One incredibly patient soul lends me her handmade papier-mâché stork whenever I hostess a baby shower, and insists on assembling my punch. She sincerely believes that although mixing sherbet and ginger ale might be duck soup for most people, one never knows about me. . . . Another talented neighbor even antiqued my old dining room table top, convinced that glamorous new surrounding would inspire me to unimagined heights of creativity. She was wrong.

In spite of my bumbling efforts, people seem to enjoy coming to our house. Perhaps it's because they are genuinely welcome, able to relax, take off their shoes, and be themselves. Perhaps it's also because the women will eventually discover my messy coat closet or gritty soap dish or fallen souffle and realize that, as hostesses, they'll have no competition from me. Whatever the reasons, we consider ourselves fortunate to have so many interesting (and tolerant) guests. I may never discover the magic formula, but it's always a thrill to hear someone say, "We had such a good time at your house. When are you guys having another party?"

Any suggestions, gals?

Sincerely,
Mrs. A.

Dear Mr. Tootle,

Just a note to let you know how interesting I found your presentation on this year's grammar school band. Actually, I have admired you from afar ever since last year's Christmas concert--any man who can successfully coordinate 27 third-grade trumpeters playing "Away in the Manger" in four completely different keys, capped by a pigtailed oboist who wet her pants during the Mistletoe March, has my undying respect.

You will note that there is a new flautist joining the band--my fourth grader. We arrived at his choice of instrument by your suggested process of elimination-- no clarinet or sax for possible orthodontia candidates, no trombones for short-armed kids, no snare drums for those with questionable coordination (or high-strung fathers) . . . actually, the flute was our only possibility. Then too, it is rather small, so Son may be able to practice in the bolted upstairs bathroom or behind the hot water heater, thus preserving the rest of the family's sanity. I realize that other mothers must have the same idea since this year's band seems to be composed of 39 flutes, a single tuba, and no drums, but it should make for an interesting effect. No?

I'm sure you'll be interested to know that our boy comes from a truly inspiring musical background. His grandmother was a child prodigy on the violin, his older brother a piano whiz (having mastered "Chopsticks" on both black-and-white keys at the tender age of four). The rest of us do a lot of group singing (sometimes even together) and his father has this intriguing tuneless whistle which filters through the house whenever he checks the overdue bill drawer. With a family history like that, I frankly expect Son to be in the band's front row by the time County Fair competition rolls around.

In any event, we have rented the flute, alterted the neighbors, and sent our toddler to Grandma's for the winter. Now there's nothing left to do but strike up the band! Best of luck to you and your ear plugs during this brave new season.

Sincerely,
Mrs. A.

Dear God,

They're on the road, many miles from home, and it's dark; it's raining. My two almost grown-up boys, so very far away. They are well-trained, responsible drivers, levelheaded and trustworthy. The car was overhauled just before their journey. And surely, everyone on the highway tonight will be cautious because of the bad weather.

So why, God, am I so terribly frightened?

Of course I know the answer, at least part of it. Friends of ours recently buried a beloved daughter, victim of a traffic accident. A young neighborhood woman has slipped into a coma, yet another statistic in the battle with cancer. A relative's child is nearing the end of his short life. Sharing grief with those who are left behind, we cannot help but be reminded of our own vulnerability, our helplessness to avoid the sorrows of this world. And we cannot help but wonder how we could bear it, could continue to go on if such an unthinkable loss touched our own lives.

Sometimes, Father, it is not enough to know that you are with us, holding us in the palm of your hand, to know that all things work together for good. Although the mind commits itself to your care, there is still the heart to be reckoned with. And hearts can be broken so quickly, so tragically. Perhaps that is what I fear most--the loss that could shatter a soul beyond repair.

And yet I have already faced these losses. From the moment I learned to love, I have also known that love might end--in rejection, yes, but also in leave taking which was no one's choice. And yet, would I have chosen a life without love, without the ties that bind us ever so closely, yet offer the possibility of pain as well?

No, God, I would not have selected such a road. Not for me the safe, uninvolved passage, free from risk but also free of growth and change--and the touching of hands and hearts. Never to have known these precious sons, never to have watched them grow, to have experienced pride and delight as they became what you and I envisioned them to be? No, Father, a thousand times no.

I have made my commitment over and over again. Each day through the myriad of happenings, large and small, I have chosen love. With all its consequences, all its possibilities, I have committed myself to love and to you, the source of it all.

So now I will sit and wait for the sound of the car in the driveway. I will be impatient, worried, frightened, yes, for my faith is not powerful enough to override my emotions. But underneath the turmoil I will know that you are here, and that together we can make it through the night.

Hold me tightly, Father, until they are home at last.

Your loving daughter

American Medical Association

Dear Sir:

I'm not overly fond of doctors' offices--the mere mention of a hypodermic needle, scale, or cotton swab usually causes me to break out in a strange rash. Nevertheless, I've spent the majority of this week's waking hours in waiting rooms, and not by choice. Several prescheduled checkups, added to a few spontaneous visits, insured five straight days of white coats and examining tables. Which was novel, of course, but not necessarily exhilarating.

One of my problems with a week like this stems not from the few minutes spent with the physician but the lifetime one is expected to spend in the physician's waiting room. A recent magazine survey concluded that patients wait an average of 32 minutes, but I suspect that poll was taken in the Sahara, for I've never experienced such a whirlwind episode. Or perhaps waiting just seems endless when one is encircled by tots sneezing streptococci germs on each other, surrounded by a bevy of young mothers playing ''Can You Top This?'' (a game requiring that gruesome symptoms or delivery room sagas be outlined in vivid detail), and is provided with only a dismal stack of torn kiddie magazines to break the monotony.

Nurses seem to take this situation in stride, I've noticed. On Monday when we'd sat in the outer office for an hour, then progressed to the inside cubicle (where they put you as part of their riot control program), I eventually summoned courage to ask the nurse if it was still autumn outside. She rolled her eyes apologetically. "It's always like this on Monday."

On Tuesday, making a return visit with another small patient, I didn't wait to count my new gray hairs, but after 90 minutes bravely inquired as to the doctor's whereabouts. Ms. Nightingale shook her head ruefully. "It's always like this on Tuesday."

Thursday's nurse (another office) seemed genuinely surprised when I used her phone to inform the sitter that I wouldn't be home for lunch. After all, I'd been at the office only since 9 AM, barely enough time to fill out the forms ("Paternal grandmother's maiden name?" "Any allergies to pizza?" "Were you recommended by a physician, a relative, a complete stranger in the supermarket checkout line?") and read some helpful literature ("The Story of Urology," "Prunes, Bran Flakes, and You") much less actually have an examination.

I realize that one of the reasons why appointment times bear no resemblance to reality is because our doctors are nice people. Because they care, they often squeeze ailing patients into an already swollen schedule or spend extra time with someone who's upset. And having been the recipient of such kindness, I see no reason to carp when the same favor is bestowed on others. But every office visit is not a three-handkerchief drama, right out of the afternoon soap operas. And although my neighbor's solution--withholding $5 per hour waiting time from her bill--seems a bit crass, I must admit I'm tempted. . . .

If doctors annoy me with their terminal tardiness, how much more must our family irritate them, however, when we finally do get together? For it is an unwritten law, at least in our domain, that the sicker a child appears (thus the more desperately urgent the appointment), the quicker his or her recovery--usually about five minutes before Dr. Bob (wearing jeans and a tank top under his whites) finally makes an appearance. Gone is Child's wan complexion, the fever, the unaccustomed listlessness. "He was very ill!" I protest as Dr. Bob, unconvinced, stares at a small body somersaulting off the examining table. (Younger Brother who, moments ago, appeared a likely candidate for Intensive Care, twirls merrily on the swivel chair.)

"Hmmmmm." Dr. Bob scoops one child onto his lap, peers into orifices, dodges a flying tongue depressor, and looks thoughtful.

"They may be coming down with flu," I offer helpfully in case (despite the diplomas lining his walls) Dr. Bob is having a bad day. "Or perhaps a bit of bronchitis."

"Hmmmm." He gives me a for-this-I-rearranged-my-whole-morning glance, grabs the younger as he darts by and subjects him to the same scrutiny. I shove Elder Brother, flushed from his romp, on the seat beside me and give him my best "Act Sick!" glower.

Tension grows. Then, "A bit of bronchitis," Dr. Bob pronounces.

"Aha!" I feel, if not vindicated, at least less neurotic. (Do they maintain a top secret office file, I wonder, with the dossiers on nervous mothers arranged in order of degree: "Somewhat Hyper," "Overly Protective," "Downright Pushy," "Hysteric"?)

"Perhaps a touch of flu, too," Dr. Bob adds, "and this boy also has ingrown toenails." It's been a real bonus day.

I wish I could say the same about the nine year old's dental checkup the following afternoon. Our dentist, a master of guilt therapy, makes certain I understand that this child is headed for gingivitis (or worse) if something isn't done soon. Dr. Phyliss knows only too well that I have committed the unpardonable Maternal Sins: 1) I've been letting the children brush without supervision, and 2) I ran out of floss last month and have been waiting for a sale.

How can I explain to this sleek all-together lady that on certain days teeth, despite their acknowledged importance, rank only fourth or fifth on my priority list, behind such activities as 1) Keeping the children from maiming themselves and/or each other, 2) Keeping the bathroom fixtures intact (or barring that, at least fastened to the wall), and 3) Keeping us from declaring bankruptcy (at least until the grade school fees from last year are paid up). It's hard to interest Dr. Phyliss in my laments, however, because as she and I both know only too well, she has our best interests at heart and is not above using scare tactics to achieve her goals.

Wearily, I drag home. At least the week is over, everyone seems healthy, and aside from a small matter of a second mortgage, the bills are paid. It's a lot to be thankful for. Quite a lot, as a matter of fact. Suddenly, I picture a world without Dr. Bob, Dr. Phyliss, penicillin, orthodontia, surgery, and a thousand other "annoyances" that help to keep us healthy and stupidly ungrateful for the miracle.

May I be stuck with type B (or even C) virus if I ever again complain!

Just thought you'd want to know.

Sincerely,
A satisfied client

October 19

Dear Ann Landers,

I never thought I'd be writing to you--especially about a problem as trivial and utterly ridiculous as this one. But my neighbor bet me two hours of baby-sitting that I wouldn't have the nerve to write, and since her kids are even worse than mine, I've decided to take the plunge.

My problem centers around our dinner hour, or lack thereof. For years my husband has held a job which requires him to work until 8 or 9 PM each evening. When the kids were little, this was no problem--I would feed them at a reasonable hour, stagger through baths, cleanup, temper tantrums (mine), and bedtime (theirs), recuperate briefly on the couch, and then whip up a new meal for Spouse and me. Much as I hate to cook, our late-night suppers actually became pleasant interludes, as we ate together with no spilled milk, and shared our news in a quiet house.

However, Ann, our children are no longer going to bed at 7 PM; in fact, they can outlast us any day of the week. My husband and I haven't had a quiet dinner since 1973. And worst of all, I'm spending the best years of my life reheating ham loaf and trying to figure out who's due to sup next. Here's a sample of what can only laughingly be referred to as our "dinner hour":

4:45 PM Feed Eldest Son who is due at work in fifteen minutes.

(He works the supper shift at a hamburger stand but must fortify his stomach before facing all that mustard.) Clean up.

5:20 PM Feed younger kids who still assume that since normal people eat at this time, they should, too. Clean up.

5:55 PM Second Son returns from after-school job; has five minutes to dine before leaving for bowling league (golf practice, sky-diving lesson). Feed, and clean up.

6:25 PM Third Son finally home from paper route collection. Feed, and clean up.

7:05 PM Eldest arrives home from supper shift at hamburger stand. Cleans up leftovers. Does not clean up kitchen.

7:30 PM Prepare snack for younger kids on way to bed. Feed, and chain them to headboards.

8:00 PM Husband arrives home, wishes to know why entire dinner has vanished, except for one tablespoon of reheated, reburned noodle casserole. Wishes to know why kitchen resembles tornado aftermath. Wishes to know why man cannot get decent meal in own home. Wishes to know why I am crying.

8:30 PM Serve new dinner to Husband. Do not speak to Husband.

10:00 PM Clean up kitchen. Plan tomorrow's dinner menu.

With a schedule like this one, Ann, I really need help. Don't tell me to use a slow cooker--I have one, and there are only two recipes that can stay intact during a five-hour meal. Don't tell me to buy a microwave oven--our kitchen is too tiny, and besides, I heard recently that they may cause warts. Don't tell me to let the kids make their own meals; I've tried that. Have you any idea how many vitamins are contained in chocolate syrup stew? (What would Dr. Phyliss say?) Or how long it takes to get scorch marks off windowsills? And don't tell me to take my husband out to dinner every night. We may run away from home.

What you can do, Ann, is tell me how to feed each member of my family a nutritious and tasty meal each evening without turning senile in the kitchen. The solution ought to be child's play for a champion problem-solver like you.

Sincerely,
Burned Up in Illinois

October 28

Dear Ann Landers,

I appreciated finding a personal response from you in my mailbox, rather than published in your column. I quite understand that it would be humiliating for you to announce publicly that you have finally discovered a problem with no solution.

Your one suggestion was interesting--however, boarding up my kitchen seems somewhat drastic, and I'm not sure the family would understand. I guess I'll just have to keep searching for delightful new hash recipes.

Thanks anyway,
Burned Up

October 31

WARNING TO ALL TRICK-OR-TREATERS (Especially those living at this address).

Now that another Halloween is upon us, kids, let's make this a safe and sane holiday. May I remind you again of the rules this "Wicked Witch of the West" expects you to honor:

1. Anyone planning to trick-or-treat as a ghost will use the old drop cloths in the garage and keep his or her mitts off my brand new flowered percales.

2. May I suggest that those dressing as bums, hobos, and other disreputable characters simply wear their everyday attire--since it horrifies me, it will probably have the same effect on other mortals.

3. My eyebrow pencil, lipstick, and other necessities are OFF LIMITS unless I am supervising makeup operation. Need I remind you of last year, when my entire cosmetic case ended up at the bottom of the toilet bowl?

4. All goblins, Donald Ducks, and fairy princesses will refrain from snitching the house candy for their own booty bags. If, however, said house candy has been depleted by supper time, Wicked Witch retains option to snitch reinforcements from aforementioned booty bags.

5. All donations to Dad's candy cache will be gratefully accepted.

6. Those attending neighborhood parties will cease all revelry by 10 PM and will refrain from splitting plastic garbage bags or ringing doorbells on their way home.

7. Bicarbonate of soda will be served promptly at 10:30 PM.

8. Taking candy along on November dentist appointments will be strictly forbidden.

Have a good time, gang--and save me some kisses (chocolate ones, that is).

Love,
The Wicked Witch

November 2

Dear Congressman,

It was a pleasure to receive your recent questionnaire--it's always nice when our elected officials ask for opinions from the voters (in postage-free envelopes), and I have many to share with you. Unfortunately, our dog has mutilated your survey, so I will forward our responses in this written note.

As to your first question, yes, we are all in favor of a strong national defense. You will be happy to know that our daughter's patriotism knows no bounds--she can hardly wait to join the Marines. (Mother may have something to say about that when the time comes, but I must admit that her karate chop is impressive.)

Yes, the recent budget cuts have hurt our personal economy--who hasn't been affected? But they're a step in the right direction. How many years have I been writing to Washington, asking you fellows to step aside and let your wives handle our country's cash flow? Our experience on the home front has taught us to avoid deficit spending by a variety of means--"Because we can't afford it, that's why!" being one of the most effective. A few years with women at the helm would result not only in a balanced national checkbook but also in a tidy sum stashed away for the proverbial rainy day (or maybe a sale on curtains for the White House kitchen). How about it?

Question Three: Are we better or worse off than we were a year ago? That's a toughie. We didn't have as many medical bills this year, but everyone's robust health led to record consumption of popcorn, apples, and pork chops (not necessarily in that order). We are all a year older, which can be positive or negative depending on who is doing the tallying. I'm better off if you consider that I'm no longer changing diapers (frankly, I thought the youngest would carry a box of disposables along to kindergarten). My spouse is worse off, if you consider that he has to paint the boys' room again this year (the previous job didn't last due to their dart tournaments). Are you considering these facts?

As to our views on transportation, may I refer you to our high school sophomore's term paper (copy enclosed) titled "What a Way to Go!" It's his contention that if the government supplied everyone (especially high school sophomores) with a free automobile, we could dismantle public transportation and put the nation to work building autos, roads, high-rise parking lots, and gas masks. Think what it would do for the economy!

Yes, Congressman, I realize there is a lot of confusion concerning your mailings to this address. It may be explained if you understand that one of our children belongs to the Student Democrats Association, another is a member of the Young Republican Club, my husband recently ordered some books from a conservative organization, and last week I attended a charismatic prayer group. In short, we do seem to confound computers--it's so difficult to file us under one political heading. Even more so, if you realize that our young Republican is currently growing a beard and learning to play "Blowin' in the Wind" on his guitar.

I trust I have cleared up your questions, and you may be sure we will all be at the polls on this upcoming election day. Whom we will vote for, however, is another story.

Sincerely,
Mrs. Constituent

November 10

Sweetheart,

Your Girl Scout cookie order arrived, and I stacked the boxes in your bedroom. Please deliver them immediately--it's almost impossible to open the door and I did want to vacuum in there before the holidays.

Some last minute adjustments to your order:

1. The lady at 411 Hickory phoned and wants two additional boxes of Do-Si-Dos. She will trade two Thin Mints with her neighbor at 413, so you won't get confused. (If I were you, I'd just dump everything on her porch and run.)

2. The couple at the end of the block have discovered that he's allergic to Tagalongs (you didn't explain about the peanut butter filling) and will either cancel or trade for two Trefoils and a Chocolate Chunk. (Take the cancellation--your dad loves Tagalongs and we can always swap our Samoas with the people in the white bungalow.)

3. Somewhere along the way you totaled the order wrong, and your scout leader is charging us for several boxes of Vanchos that never arrived. Can you clear this up, Honey, before Mother goes completely gray?

Don't forget the camp-out this weekend--be sure to pack your mess kit, kerchief, and sleeping bag this time. (And you might want to take those extra boxes of Vanchos along to share around the campfire.)

Let me know when I can enter your room.

Mom

Dear Carol,

Yes, our eldest son did get off to college on schedule, and it was really sweet of you to be concerned. I imagine, as manager of our local teen hangout, you've seen lots of kids exiting for the halls of higher learning, but it was a first for me, and something I will never forget. The logistics of packing, for instance. Who would have imagined that eight pairs of blue jeans, six flannel shirts, and several toeless sneakers could be compressed into a 10'' x 24'' duffel bag? Or that our car trunk could hold a small stereo (boy, was I glad to see that go!), my best electric frying pan (smuggled out in a pillow case), and an easy chair (its absence not noticed until Husband decided to sit in it)?

Then there was the unloading, with parents passing dirty looks back and forth as each family vied for limited elevator space (who wants to carry an easy chair up to the sixth floor?). And bearded upperclassmen standing around in raggy cutoffs, eating cold baked beans out of cans, and eyeing the most promising freshman girls. (True to form, Son had neglected to mention his dorm was coed.) And handling a wealth of papers, registration forms, books lists. And wandering through the campus, gazing at the new world that our son is joining, and wondering if we have raised him well enough to cope. . . .

And driving home, just the two of us, in a car that seemed far too empty.

Son has been home a few times since then, and I do think I'm beginning to get the hang of being a college student's parent. For one thing, offspring never come home alone. There is always a Frank or Freddy (sometimes even a Frieda) who needs a pad "just for tonight, Ma--he'll sleep anywhere, honest!" and who will then be picked up by yet another car, on another lap of his convoluted route homeward.

Today's kids, I've noticed, are quite casual about the classes they choose. They study just as hard as their parents did, but the course offerings have been widened so dramatically that it's almost impossible to make an informed selection.

"You're taking 'Existential Relationships and Aspects of the Id'?" I asked Son.

He shrugged. "Sounds interesting."

"And 'Statistics and Dynamics on the Linear Square'?"

"Sure, why not?"

"'Introduction to Badminton'?"

"Yup."

As long as I can decipher the report card, does it really matter?

I've also noticed that CARE packages from home are as mandatory as prompt tuition payments. Said parcels should contain cookies and brownies (preferably homemade), fruit (a word of caution--grapes do not pack well), meat sticks, and yet another can opener. (I think kids eat can openers.) And if a few greenbacks of varying denominations are tucked among the navel oranges, no student will object.

Yes, Carol, it's been a real educational experience for Mom as well as Son. I'm sure he's looking forward to telling you all about it when he's home for Thanksgiving break. I'm buying an extra-large turkey in case Frank or Frieda accompanies him, and Husband is planning a sneak attack on Son's duffel bag to recover his electric razor.

See you soon,
Mrs. A.

Dear Family,

In between searching for my red-and-yellow turkey platter (did I hide it in the crawl space last November? in the linen closet? under my bed?) and persuading Aunt Betty that it is her turn to bring dessert for thirty, I try to take time each Thanksgiving to be grateful. For . . .

A husband who tolerates my mid-life crises (which I've been having regularly since I turned 25), who has learned to ignore dust, and can cope with the sight of blood.

A teenager so thrilled with his new driver's license that he will cheerfully chauffeur my kindergarten carpool or pick up the dry cleaning at a moment's notice.

One-sided newspaper editorials, especially when they represent my point of view.

Garage sales, which allow me to recycle my junk into the neighbors' houses (until they host a sale and recycle it all back).

A son who did not try out for the football team this year, and who regards all contact sports as hazardous to his retainer brace.

Supermarkets that stock convenience foods (for moms who regard cooking as one step removed from the torture chamber) and occasionally run sales on luxuries such as laundry detergent and meat.

Grandmothers, especially those who pop in unexpectedly, survey the ruins and the harried look in Daughter's eyes, and suggest kindly, "Why don't I take the children out for a walk?"

Grandfathers, especially those who, while observing

their son making a fool of himself with levels and saws, resist the impulse to suggest, "Why don't you give in and call a carpenter?"

School Lost-and-Found departments, which make me realize that things at our house aren't as disorganized as I thought. While I search for a sweater, I can wonder what sort of children misplace an ant farm, encyclopedia volumes A through E, and an accordian.

A young daughter who sings constantly and cheerfully, even though her repertoire is limited to "Hang Down Your Head, Tom Dooley."

The fact that no one in our family developed ingrown toenails, plague, athlete's foot, diphtheria, tetanus, whooping cough, or dandruff this year.

Pets, especially those who stay in the same place for long periods or, barring that, are the sole responsibility of someone else.

Friends I can phone on "one of those days," and who will say sympathetically, "Just let me catch the hamster, wipe up the water from all these flooded pipes, and find my coffee cup--then you can tell me all about it."

The last pair of scissors in the house, which no one will confiscate because it is hidden in my pantyhose.

My husband's dinner table lectures to the kids, including "How many times must I tell you to (close the refrigerator door, stop taking seven showers a day, don't warm marshmallows in the clothes drier, stay away from my tool bench)," and "The next time I find your bike in the driveway, I'm going to . . . ."

Other people's two year olds, especially when they throw screaming fits in church, the pediatrician's office, and the supermarket checkout line. It's nice to know my own pint-sized monster is perfectly normal.

And God, who (for reasons best known to him) accepts my foibles and loves me, anyway.

Yes, gang, I'm grateful, for no-iron shirts and

sunshine and quiet walks and freedom and the sweet fragrance of just-washed hair. For little kids who like to cuddle, and big kids who'll still endure a maternal hug now and then. For a large extended family who makes Thanksgiving a time of joy and sharing and blissful reunion. For life lived, if not perfectly, at least to the fullest.

And especially for the fact that there are at least 30 more shopping days til Christmas.

Now, if any of you guys has discovered my red-and-yellow turkey platter, please let me know.

Love,
Mom

December 7

Dear Jim,

Sorry I missed your service call--I'd been summoned to school for an emergency meeting (something will have to be done about the fourth grader's habit of climbing onto roofs!). Anyway, I've left a check--just fill in the amount, as usual.

As to the problems, you will notice that the washing machine seems to move across the floor during the spin cycle, accompanied by a sound similar to castanets. I thought this was due to an imbalanced load, but after I removed the teenager's nine pair of jeans (and several of his father's used-to-be-white shirts), the bumps and grinds continued. I can only conclude that:

   a) The machine loves to dance.
   b) There are castanets in the drain hose.
   c) The fan belt is shot.
   d) My husband will be angry about his shirts.
   e) All of the above.
   f) (Fill in your own diagnosis.)

The drier is behaving much more calmly, except that it simply refuses to dry the clothes. They drift around in there for ages with no noticeable improvement. I thought matters might start to improve when I removed the stale toast that Daughter was trying to warm up, but it didn't work. Since my husband took down my clothes line during his autumn clean-up-the-yard campaign, this situation is making life difficult for all of us. I can only conclude that:

   a) The machine prefers raisin toast.
   b) The lint filter is blocked, due to crumbs.
   c) We use the drier too often.

d) The fan belt is shot.

e) My husband will be angry about this bill.

f) All of the above.

g) (Fill in your own diagnosis.)

If you have time, Jim, or your wife doesn't expect you home for dinner, could you take a look at the dishwasher? It's been spitting soapsuds on the floor for over a week. I can only conclude that:

a) The kids filled it with bubble bath instead of detergent.

b) I ought to make the kids do the dishes by hand until they get married.

c) My husband isn't going to speak to me for a week.

It's wonderful to have all these modern appliances, isn't it? If only they would work!

Do your best, Jim. And enjoy your Florida vacation, compliments of the Anderson family.

Mrs. A.

December 10

Dear Relatives and Friends,

A warm and wonderful holiday season to you all. Tis the time for mistletoe, holly, and the Anderson family's annual newsletter enclosed, as usual, in our Christmas card. (Please excuse the design--Husband chose the cards this year, and while I would have preferred something more sedate--a manger scene, perhaps, or a choir of angels--I suppose a polar bear wearing a NOEL neck wreath does have a certain charm.)

At any rate, on to the family news. We know you'll be delighted to hear that our high school freshman traveled to Florida this past spring with his marching band, which won top honors in the national competition. (Son didn't get a chance to play, unfortunately; he inadvertently locked himself in the hotel bathroom during the performance).

Husband has been keeping busy pursuing his hobbies--napping, watching TV, and answering the phone. Mom took an Honorable Mention at the Park District pot holder competition this year, and also managed to match up all the socks. Daughter swam across the pool without stopping. Second Son changed a light bulb, and our youngest learned to cross the street alone. Two of the teens passed their driving tests, we've wallpapered the kitchen, and discovered that the house needs a new sewer line. All in all, a most eventful year, wouldn't you agree?

Have a wonderful Christmas, and keep in touch!

Love,
Us

December 12

Buy basketball for Chris.
Raisins for oatmeal cookies.
Butter for butter cookies.
Chocolate chips for chocolate chip cookies.
(Maybe consider bakery cookies?)
Check tinsel supply.
Would Spouse like dress shirt?
Mail packages to Jay, Audrey, David, Theresa, Betty.
    (Brown paper? String? Stamps?)
Get sub for playground duty at junior high.
Laundry.
Cough syrup, cold tablets, aspirin, nasal spray, ear
    drops. Call pediatrician.
Replace candles on Advent wreath.

December 16

Note double schedule of choir rehearsals.
Phone call to guests for Christmas dinner (Commit
    Grandma for gravy making).
Exchange basketball for baseball and mitt for Chris.
Gifts for bridge club party.
Red bow for band concert uniform.
Would Spouse like bathrobe?
Library books due Monday.
Try new spot remover on lace tablecloth. Investigate
    paper tablecloth.
Laundry.
Cancel dentist appointment.

December 19

Exchange baseball for football.
Batteries and wrapping paper. Scotch tape.
Paper tablecloth.
Would Spouse like slacks?
Shop Tuesday for family groceries. Shop Thursday for
   Christmas groceries. Shop Friday for forgotten
   groceries.
Lamb's costume for kindergarten play?
Teachers' gifts.
Pick up choir robe. Iron.
Borrow vaporizer.
Whipped cream? Sour cream? Coffee cream? Cold
   cream? Creme de menthe?
Replace damaged ornaments. Set up tree again.

December 23

Exchange football for hockey stick for Chris.
Set table, find extra chairs in garage. Repair chairs.
Start making ice cubes.
Defrost turkey.
Post work schedule for kids.
Would Spouse like portable radio?
Rug cleaner? Scouring powder? Stain remover?
   Furniture polish? Restaurant reservations?
Return puppy. Fourth grader isolated in bedroom.
Laundry.
Casseroles? Hors d'oeuvres? Relishes? Rolls? Razor
   blades?
Water poinsettia.
Bake birthday cake for Baby Jesus.
Do not lose this list!
Pray!

===

Dear Diary,

It's New Year's Eve. Time to ring out the old,
welcome the new--and make another list of resolutions.
I don't need to compile one, however. I've got a
perfectly good list left from last year because I didn't
accomplish anything on it. Yet, strangely, even though
I forgot to take up aerobic dance, bleach my hair,
master patience and humility, or learn to speak
French, I still feel a sense of fulfillment.

For one thing, I've made it through another year,
and I like this stage in life. The "baby days," full of
exhausting physical demands, have waned but the
household is still humming, crammed with the sounds
of an active and comfortable group, my favorite people.
I'm beginning to understand the real rewards of
parenthood now as I watch the seeds of my long-ago
labors blossom into offspring of whom I can be
rightfully proud. Motherhood is such an intangible
journey; we deal in the language of the heart with few
road signs, report cards, or guarantees along the way.
And yet, if we manage to persevere, there is no
"tangible" in all the world that can equal our reward.

I like this phase of marriage, too. Over two decades
spent in hammering out compromises, discarding
juvenile behavior for the cloak of maturity (which
often slips, despite our good intentions), and merging
two diverse personalities into common accord have led
to a closeness that I wouldn't have understood as a
bride. There are days when I wonder what a nice
person like me is doing in a zoo like this. But there are
more days when I wonder what I'd do without any of
them, but especially him.

I'm living as a "middle ager" now, and it's a satisfied, somehow settled feeling. Gone are the naive dreams of a "someday" when everything will become organized, understood, predictable. Instead I've learned to rejoice in the present moment, imperfect but precious because it will never come again. It's been a slow, groping process, this emerging maturity, but a welcome development. Life lived one day at a time can be immensely satisfying, surprisingly free. And if growing up means adding a few pounds, wrinkles (we call them laugh lines), or gray hairs, I'll gladly make the trade.

Yes, Diary, the world keeps spinning, but somehow I'm still hanging on. The essentials of life, I'm discovering, cannot be supplied--or taken away--by outward trappings, impressive achievement, or roles. They spring, like most worthwhile things, from within a woman's heart.

So I won't need a new list of resolutions after all, Diary, nor tin horns and champagne to mark another milestone. Instead, the celebration goes on every day, deep within me. I love, and I am loved. It is enough, for this year and for all those to follow.

Happy New Year, Diary. Let's see what it brings, together. There are still lots of pages left in my little white book.

Love,
Me